T0361603

POOR CHOICES AND UNRESOLVED
TRAUMA IS KILLING AMERICA

# A LIFE
# FOR A
# LIFE

## KEVIN SHIRD

Post Hill
PRESS

*To Brenda Mills and Joi Crosby*

# TABLE OF CONTENTS

# PROLOGUE

*Summer 1999*
*Jerome Avenue*
*Bronx, New York City*

IT WAS NEARLY NINE O'CLOCK on a warm summer evening in the Bronx, one of New York City's five boroughs. As I strolled down Jerome Avenue with my business partner, the screeching of an elevated subway train echoed as it raced along the metal tracks above. To my right, a Latina mother stood at a bus stop, holding her child's hand while discreetly clutching a sharp razor blade concealed in her purse. A cautious Catholic priest walked by, carrying a Bible under his arm and rosary beads in his hand, making the sign of the cross over his cassock robe. On the opposite side of the street, Russian mobsters loitered in front of a curbside carwash, engrossed in conversations on their Motorola flip phones. Their watchful eyes kept close tabs on both their expensive foreign cars being washed and polished and the illicit businesses in the vicinity. This gritty environment exuded tension and menace, but it was home to the people who lived there.

As my partner and I continued down the bustling boulevard, teenagers played double-Dutch in the middle of the street, accompanied by the booming sound of Jennifer Lopez's latest hit record blaring from the neighborhood's loudest radio. Latinas with long black hair bobbed their heads to the music, seated on stoops lining the block as far as the eye could see.

As we proceeded down Jerome Avenue, the tantalizing aroma of Dominican rice cooking on a nearby stove fanned through the air. The mouthwatering spices, undoubtedly imported from the Caribbean, were irresistible. If you hadn't appreciated Dominican food before, one whiff of this would surely change your mind.

Waiting at a red light on the corner, about to cross 152nd Street in the distance, we had a view of the iconic Yankee Stadium to our left. It was the place where Babe Ruth had become a baseball legend playing for the New York Yankees. But the game my partner and I were playing on this warm summer night wasn't baseball, and we couldn't afford to strike out.

Our contact went by the name of Diego, but in this underground drug economy, you never really knew who these people were. Almost everyone involved in this part of town had a fake name and a counterfeit identification card to match. Diego, a tall Dominican with tattoos and a constant Marlboro cigarette in his mouth, had a thick accent that suggested he hadn't been in the States for very long.

Upon arriving at the corner of 161st Street, we stopped at a payphone and called Diego. "We're here." My business partner still had his blue backpack slung over his left shoulder, loaded with US currency. Within fifteen minutes, a dark-navy-blue gypsy cab pulled up to the curb, and we climbed inside. Our driver, an elderly Latino gentleman with gray streaks in his hair, likely a Cuban immigrant, sported an "I love Fidel" T-shirt and smoked a Cohiba Cuban cigar. After departing from the pickup location, we passed through Fordham Road and over the Bronx River Parkway into an even tougher neighborhood.

Diego and two Dominican associates were waiting for us in front of the King Dragon Chinese food takeout joint on Randall Avenue. One of Diego's companions had a rough six-inch scar on his left cheek, while the other man walked with a noticeable limp. These were the marks of individuals who had been through some rough places and back again.

"Yo, what's up? How's the *familia*?" Diego inquired.

"Everybody's good, bro," I responded.

It had been a long day, and exhaustion and hunger were setting in. All I wanted at that moment was to conclude our business and return home.

"Aren't you going to introduce me to your homeboy?" Diego asked.

"What's up, bro?" my partner replied.

"These are my cousins, Gino and Manny. They just arrived from Santo Domingo with my uncle. I'll need to introduce you to him someday," Diego remarked.

"Where is he?"

"In the hospital. His face and arm were burned pretty bad in a fire." Deigo said.

After a short walk down Rosedale Avenue, we reached the gritty Soundview housing projects. Three elderly women were pushing small laundry carts down the sidewalk, returning from the laundromat, while Latin kids played skully on a chalk-drawn board in the middle of the street. As we entered the building, we boarded a rickety elevator that took us to the sixth floor, where street guys stood in the hallway, handguns concealed under their shirts. They were prepared to do the unthinkable for a price few sane individuals could comprehend. The walls seemed to whisper, sharing dark secrets about the hallways. Shortly thereafter, an unsettling sensation washed over me, signaling trouble. I had made this trip dozens of times for transactions like these, but this visit felt different.

As we entered a nondescript apartment, I noticed two weapons resting on a coffee table. One was a black nine-millimeter handgun, and the other, a silver .357 revolver with a rubber grip handle. Both were tools of the trade. The nine-millimeter was the preferred firearm for the average street shooter, while the revolver was the coveted weapon of an experienced assassin.

"So, how's the family, bro?"

Our host repeated the same question for the second time in fifteen minutes. It was more small talk from a typically business-minded individual.

"My family is good, man," I replied as my partner placed his blue backpack on the table, revealing the cash inside. "Let's count this money so we can get out of here," I urged.

"Okay, okay, brother. I got you," Diego responded with a smile. Moments later, his cell phone rang, and he answered it.

"Hola?"

Glancing at the wall clock, I noted that it was exactly ten thirty—perfect timing, I thought to myself. Following his brief conversation in Spanish, Diego turned to my partner and I and said, "I need to run downstairs for a minute. My cousins will take care of you."

That's when Diego exited the apartment, closing the door behind him, and chaos erupted inside. Gino and Manny swiftly grabbed the two weapons from the coffee table and declared, "You know what time it is! Put your fucking hands up, and nobody gets hurt. I'm serious, *do it*!"

Gino was the more aggressive of the two assailants, and he seemed to be the one we needed to be most concerned about. "Manny, get the tape. *Agarrar la cuerda*," he ordered. Manny, younger and more apprehensive, was still equally culpable in this dangerous situation.

Just minutes earlier, I'd had a nagging sense of unease about the situation, and it turned out my instincts had been right. It was as if the scent of betrayal was hanging in the air, and the Game Gods were sending a warning about Diego's intentions.

Gino instructed us to sit in chairs across from each other, and then they began to bind us with duct tape. At that moment, Manny bent over to retrieve another roll of tape from the floor and accidentally dropped his gun. Seeing an opportunity, I lunged for the weapon and ended up on the floor, engaged in a fierce struggle. My partner also seized the moment and grappled with Gino, attempting to disarm him. I knew that someone was likely to die in this desperate struggle, and I prayed it wouldn't be me.

As Manny and I wrestled on the floor, I struck him in the chin, momentarily dazing him. He was as strong as an ox. I hit him again, this time in the neck, causing him to gasp for air. Then, I reached for the .357 Magnum revolver, gripping it by the handle. My partner was unable to overpower Gino, who discharged the nine-millimeter from across the room. As the hot lead tore through my upper body, I clutched my chest, experiencing the most excruciating pain I had ever felt. Gino fired a second round, striking me in the shoulder. The projectile, traveling at 600 mph, tore through my flesh as easy as a razor slicing through a stick of butter. That's when death began to tighten its grip around me. My Uber ride to either heaven or hell had arrived, offering a one-way ticket to the afterlife. But if I was leaving this world, I was determined to take someone with me.

Blood dripped from my nose as I locked eyes with Gino and aimed for his center mass. In that moment, I envisioned him playing with his dog in the backyard, then walking down the aisle with his beautiful bride at his wedding. Finally, I imagined him lying in a casket, dressed in a cheap suit, surrounded by grieving gang members vowing revenge.

"Papi, please don't," were Gino's last words as the deafening gunshot filled the apartment.

Then, suddenly...I woke up!

It had all been just another terrifying nightmare. I was actually at home, lying in my bed when I came out of the dream. Sweat poured from my brow, and my hand trembled. The illusion had been so vivid that I instinctively reached for my chest, searching for a wound, but fortunately, there was none.

For two decades, I had been haunted by these dreadful nightmares of being violently injured or murdered. Sometimes they would fade away for extended periods, only to return with a vengeance. These were the mental scars I carried from the traumatic events I had endured while involved in street life, and even years later, they continued to plague me. This was the residue of unresolved trauma, and it seemed that my undiagnosed post-traumatic stress disorder was still very much a part of my life, rearing its head in the form of these vivid dreams. The world-renowned Johns Hopkins Hospital describes the disorder this way: "you may have post-traumatic stress disorder (PTSD) if you've been through a traumatic event and are having trouble dealing with it. Such events may include a car crash, rape, domestic violence, military combat, or violent crime. While it is normal to have anxiety after such an event, it usually goes away with time. But with PTSD, the anxiety becomes more intense and keeps coming back. And the trauma is relived through nightmares, intrusive memories, and flashbacks (vivid memories that seem real). The symptoms of PTSD can cause problems with relationships and make it hard to cope with daily life. But it can be treated."[1]

An estimated one in eleven people will be diagnosed with PTSD in their lifetime. I just happen to be one of them. Today, I am a writer, activist, advocate, and social entrepreneur. The rocky waters I navigated just to arrive at a place of normalcy where my talents could blossom were treacherous. But the wealth of knowledge I have to share with the world of academia, literature, and policy are endless, and probably wouldn't have been obtained without my journey through darkness.

---

1    "Posttraumatic Stress Disorder (PTSD)," Johns Hopkins Medicine, https://www.hopkinsmedicine.org/health/conditions-and-diseases/posttraumatic-stress-disorder-ptsd. Accessed September 8, 2024.

# CHAPTER 1

# THE DEPARTED

*Fall 2002*
*Edward A. Garmatz United States District Courthouse*
*Baltimore, Maryland*

I FOUND MYSELF IN A small prisoner holding cell at the courthouse, switching between sitting, standing, and pacing around. The morning had been tough, as I had just been sentenced on drug trafficking charges, and my life had been turned upside down once again. In this environment, showing no sign of weakness to those around you was important. Although I hadn't slept well the night before, I had to maintain the facade of strength. I needed to convey to others that everything was okay—and that I was immune to the agony of incarceration.

Nobody I knew enjoyed returning to prison, not even those who pretended they didn't care. Perhaps there was a lunatic somewhere who couldn't wait to get back to Cell Block D, where Oodles of Noodles and homemade wine made from rotten oranges were the norm. But for those of us who had experienced that dark place, as close to hell as you could get without being inside the devil's den, there was no excitement about returning.

The federal courthouse cellblock was a dismal place with dingy gray walls that seemed to numb your spirit. The moment you entered, the stench of imprisoned men decaying and wasting away assaulted your nostrils. The drizzly morning had obscured the small amount of sunlight that usually trickled through the windows, casting the cellblock into further darkness.

As the afternoon approached, hunger gnawed at me. Brown paper bags containing bologna-and-cheese sandwiches, accompanied by bags of stale potato chips, leftovers from the Gulf War, were strewn on the bench in my cell. Few detainees wanted anything to do with those meals because everyone knew that feeding court detainees bound for the penitentiary was a low priority for the government. It was painfully evident.

The cellblock was usually quiet, punctuated only by the occasional jingling of keys. This was a sign that a prisoner was either headed to the courtroom or returning to their cell with a stiff sentence handed down by a Republican judge. When you were being sentenced for a federal crime, you were usually looking at a harsh mandatory minimum sentence. Detainees oftentimes had their spirits broken once they'd met the judge's gaze.

I was in the middle of eating a stale bologna sandwich when I heard a commotion down the hall. Earlier that morning, rumors had circulated about the notorious DC Sniper, also known as the Beltway Sniper. The rumor had it that he and his accomplice were appearing in court for a hearing. These two were the most wanted men in America at the time, having been arrested a few days earlier in Western Maryland, where they'd been found in their infamous black Chevy Caprice with heavily tinted windows. Prior to their capture, law enforcement officials across multiple states had been pursuing them.

Allegedly, these two had been driving across the country, shooting innocent people from a sniper nest constructed inside the trunk of their car. At the time of their arrest, they faced charges from law enforcement officials in Maryland, Virginia,

Georgia, Alabama, and Louisiana. They were in federal court that morning for an extradition hearing, which would determine the order in which they would be transferred to different states to stand trial.

I was engrossed in the drama watching from my cell when I saw one of the snipers for the first time. There he was, live and in the flesh, surrounded by heavily armed US marshals. It felt surreal. I could only imagine what was going through his mind as he walked through a maze of federal agents, all clad in bulletproof vests and camouflage outfits, carrying lethal weapons. This was the first time I had seen federal officers inside the cellblock with firearms. Guns were typically restricted, but this was a special occasion, and they weren't taking chances. Any false move by either prisoner would result in maximum force being deployed against them. The tables had turned, and the two guests were no longer wolves hunting innocent prey; they were now sheep waiting to be devoured.

The first of the two prisoners to walk down the narrow hallway was Lee Boyd Malvo. He wore a bright orange prison jumpsuit and white tennis shoes provided by his new jailers. Malvo stood about five-foot-three and appeared to weigh around 120 pounds. The first thought that crossed my mind when I saw him was how news reports had identified him as a seventeen-year-old. He looked even younger than that, like a teenager who could blend in at any high school cafeteria in America. He didn't come across as menacing. In fact, he seemed to be perplexed by his new surroundings.

Malvo was about twenty feet away from my cell when the marshals began escorting him in my direction. I moved closer to the cell bars to get a better look. His feet were shackled, making it difficult for him to maneuver down the corridor. When he locked eyes with me, I couldn't help but think, *Welcome to hell.*

After Malvo was placed in the empty cell to my right, the marshals slammed the cell door shut and turned their attention to John Allen Muhammed, the alleged mastermind. As Muhammad walked into the hallway, I had the opportunity to get a closer look at him. He didn't resemble the terrorist portrayed in the evening news. Instead, he could easily pass for a high school basketball coach or an average guy shopping for holiday gifts at the mall. He stood at about five-foot-seven and weighed around 160 pounds. News sources had reported Muhammad's age as forty-two, but he looked much younger. He didn't appear to be a vicious killer, but his deceptive appearance might have been one of the reasons he had remained elusive.

After being searched, Muhammad was escorted to the far end of the cellblock, to a prison cell far away from Malvo. The two alleged killers were celebrities of sorts, but for all the wrong reasons. This wasn't Hollywood, and if they were convicted, they would pay a tremendous price.

From his cell at the other end of the cellblock, Muhammad began yelling at the top of his voice. "Lee Boyd! Lee Boyd! You okay?"

Malvo responded in an unyielding Jamaican accent, "I'm good, man. I'm okay."

"This is bullshit, man," Muhammad said, breaking into laughter. "We're gonna get out of here. Don't worry! Don't worry!"

Malvo's response lacked the same enthusiasm as his accomplice's. He sounded drained and more attuned to the harsh reality of his situation. That is when it dawned on me that due to the seriousness of his crimes, this young teenager might never see the streets again. Listening to their conversation, I wondered if Muhammad was naive or perhaps the most narcissistic person I had ever come across. He spoke as if he were enjoying the moment and would be going home to celebrate. Did Muhammad realize he would never walk out of those doors alive, or was he putting on a show to comfort his young co-defendant, knowing that both their days were numbered? For a year, these two individuals had been anonymous to the world. However, their capture had lifted the veil on their identities and exposed their nefarious activities. I couldn't fathom what the other inmates felt about them, but I had witnessed how these situations played out before. When a high-profile prisoner enters any prison, there's usually a grace period during which they intrigue the general population. But that period is often followed by the realization that they are just regular guys, imprisoned like the rest of us.

I had been around violent guys connected to the mafia, drug cartels, and even spies charged with espionage. I remember being on the cellblock with Ted Kaczynski, also known as the Unabomber, a man who had sent bombs through the mail to twenty-six people. I had been around some of the most violent men imaginable, but something was different about these two. The level of violence they had inflicted on innocent people was troubling. This was the calculated murder of ten innocent people and the wounding of three others.

The most heinous incident they were accused of committing during their nationwide shooting spree was when they waited outside of a middle school in Maryland and shot a thirteen-year-old student in the chest. A pediatric surgeon testified in court about how he had helped to repair the victim's damaged organs during emergency surgery. The bullet had shredded the young boy's body, and the damage was massive.

Friends of mine who worked in Washington, DC, during their crime spree told me that they were afraid to walk to their cars after leaving their offices because they were worried about being shot by the anonymous killers. Others told me that they didn't want to leave their homes because they were afraid of becoming the next victim. I remember a friend telling me that one day a car backfired in downtown Washington, DC, and she watched as crowds of people ran for cover. America had been traumatized by two serial killers bent on terrorizing the nation. I wonder how many people are still dealing with mental health issues as a result of those events. I wonder how many sought counseling and how many of them still have trouble sleeping at night.

In the weeks that followed, I would witness the transformation of the DC Snipers' fame from notoriety to obscurity. The inmates would learn that these men were no different from the rest of us, locked behind bars with no special privileges. They were confined to their cells, just like the rest of us, and the hype surrounding them would soon subside. This was the harsh reality of life in prison: your past deeds, no matter how infamous, could not protect you from the monotony and harsh conditions of incarceration.

I couldn't help but think about the choices we all make in life and how they lead us to our own individual fates. The DC Snipers, once feared and elusive killers, were now confined to a small, dimly lit cellblock, awaiting their trials and the justice that would be served to them. It was a sobering reminder that in the end, our actions have consequences, and no one, no matter how clever or notorious, is immune.

In prison, where time moves slowly and the days blend together, I often found myself reflecting on the choices that had brought me here and the path that lay ahead. The journey was far from over, and as I watched the DC Snipers fade into the background of prison life, I couldn't help but wonder what the future held for all of us.

Following court proceedings that afternoon, all detainees who were not released on bond were transported to the detention center. It was the normal procedure that followed daily court hearings and jury trials. Around 4:30 p.m. about two dozen federal detainees were loaded into transport vans for the short drive to the nearby detention center known as the supermax. The supermax was a high security prison facility located about two miles from the courthouse. It was once described as one of the most escape-proof prisons in America.

Muhammad and Malvo were placed in a blue van with dark tinted windows. As we exited the courthouse garage in a van behind theirs, I noticed teams of snipers on the rooftop of the courthouse and some surrounding buildings. These government agents were dressed in all black. They held long rifles with sight scopes attached which could zero in on any target they felt was a threat. The government was not taking any chances.

Pratt Street is a very busy street found just behind the courthouse, and it was blocked off for several blocks by law enforcement officials driving in unmarked cars. The prisoner transport vans were given free rein and were traveling at least forty miles an hour. Loaded with valuable cargo, they continued nonstop past the Inner Harbor tourists until they reached President Street.

A few weeks later, I saw on the news that Muhammad and Malvo had been taken to Virginia to face prosecution. Virginia was the state seasoned law enforcement officials wanted the pair extradited to first because the commonwealth state has one of the toughest death penalty laws in the country. The prosecutors there knew that if the pair were convicted at trial, they would never leave Virginia alive and the other states that wanted to prosecute them would have to do it in the afterlife.

After spending about a month in the supermax, I was handcuffed and shackled by the US marshals, along with several other prisoners, and transported to Virginia. Our destination was the Northern Neck Regional Jail in Warsaw. Northern Neck was another detention center that held federal detainees after sentencing and until they were transferred to the massive Federal Bureau of Prisons system to serve their time. Many of the guards at Northern Neck displayed obnoxious, disrespectful behavior, making it clear they held no regard for inmates' needs. The atmosphere reeked of hatred, and racial tensions were overt and undeniable. Surviving there meant staying off the radar until you reached your next destination. You didn't need to be a punk, but you had to be smart when dealing with correctional officers prone to violence. Why? Because the last thing anyone wanted was a physical altercation with a guard leading to another "accidental" death.

All inmates housed in Northern Neck wore black-and-white-striped prison uniforms that seemed right out of the 1920s, reminiscent of a time when prisoners in the South picked cotton in the bayou. On the bright side, the facility was relatively clean, a stark contrast to the supermax facility in Baltimore, where spending the entire night battling roaches was the norm.

It was at Northern Neck Regional Jail that I first met Damion "Soul" Neal, an inmate from a tough East Baltimore neighborhood. He initially appeared serene and easygoing, but it didn't take long for me to realize he was not someone to trifle with. Damion was one of fourteen inmates assigned to four large prison cells inside the housing unit. I slept on the bottom bunk closest to the door, while Damion occupied a bunk in the corner at the other end. The mattresses were barely three inches thick, offering minimal support. Of course, comfort was a luxury in Virginia, where the constant uncertainty of unexpected incidents during the night kept me on edge. The slightest sound would jolt me awake, even if it turned out to be nothing. Vigilance was paramount, especially when sharing sleeping quarters with several inmates, as conflicts could easily escalate to violence while you slept, often with no warning.

Damion and I bonded over our shared connection to Baltimore. Whether discussing the city's sports teams, like football and baseball, or legendary cooking specialties, like

Maryland crab cakes, our conversations flowed naturally. In a prison environment, the designation of being "homeboys" from the same town carried weight.

"Which part of the city are you from?" I asked.

"The east side, near Chester Street. What about you?" Damion replied.

"I lived in Edmondson Village when I was young, but we moved around a few times. How long you been here?"

"Two weeks. I just got sentenced," he replied.

"What were you convicted for?"

"One of those 924G handgun charges," Damion explained.

Damion's criminal case had started as a state matter, involving illegal handgun possession. The state prosecutor later transferred his case to the United States Attorney's Office, making it a federal court matter.

"I didn't even know what a 924G was until the FBI arrested me while I was leaving state court. The state dismissed the case, and the feds picked it up. I was like, 'Wait a minute. I'm with the state. I don't have no damn federal case.' They took me right downtown to the federal building and re-charged me with the same handgun," Damion recounted.

Baltimore, like many other cities, grappled with its illegal gun culture. Programs like Project Exile, a partnership between the US Attorney's Office and the Baltimore City Police Department, aimed to address the issue by sending those arrested for illegal handgun possession to federal prison. It was a comprehensive strategy to combat gun violence, but its effectiveness remained debatable.

Northern Neck Regional Jail, located in a rural area of Northern Virginia, housed mostly inmates from the surrounding regions. While the inmates from Baltimore and Washington, DC, tended to be more aggressive, the locals were generally less confrontational, but respect remained essential.

Most of the Baltimore inmates incarcerated there were dispersed throughout different housing units. In addition to Damion, there was another Baltimore native in my unit, Maurice. Hailing from the west side of town, Maurice had a reputation for being reckless and confrontational. He had recently been sentenced to five years in federal prison for illegal handgun possession, a charge similar to Damion's. Maurice's loudmouthed and unpredictable behavior often led to clashes with both guards and fellow inmates, making him someone to be cautious around.

The housing unit had a single television that fifty-six inmates had to share. In Virginia, news coverage of the DC Sniper case dominated the airwaves. The constant media attention on the two accused killers, who had been extradited to Virginia and housed at Northern Neck, was hard to escape. They were kept in protective custody to ensure their safety, as their convictions and executions were a top priority for authorities. Details of their heinous crimes slowly emerged, revealing a disturbing pattern. Law enforcement officials discovered that Muhammad had been shooting innocent people around the country just to create a distraction. Allegedly, the scheme was for him to assassinate his estranged wife and have a nameless sniper blamed for her murder. Then, he would regain custody of his children and walk away as the grieving husband.

One evening, tensions flared when Maurice nearly got into a fight with an inmate over control of the television. This inmate was from Virginia and wanted to watch the local news, while Maurice insisted on ESPN for the latest sports scores and highlights. The argument escalated, but eventually, the Virginia inmate conceded, allowing Maurice to have his way.

"Screw you," Maurice said.

"Look, man, ain't nobody trying to rumble over no television."

The inmate from Virginia argued back and forth with Maurice for a few minutes, but then, he let him have his way with the state-owned idiot box.

I spent much of my time in Northern Neck playing chess with fellow inmates. I had picked up the game a few months earlier, and it quickly became an obsession. Chess provided a mental escape from the prison environment, allowing me to focus and block out the noise around me. In the game of chess, the queen, like in life, held immense power, capable of dominating the board. And like in real life, each move carried the potential for victory or defeat.

One day, as I was deeply engrossed in a game of chess, I witnessed Maurice engage in yet another altercation, this time with eight inmates over watching the television.

"If I can't watch what I want to watch, ain't nobody watching nothing!" Then, he picked up the television and, in slow motion, tossed it onto the concrete floor.

*Crash!*

As the Samsung slammed onto the hard floor, the screen shattered into a million small pieces. Even the sociopaths in the housing unit were stunned.

"What the hell?" an inmate yelled.

The sudden act of destruction triggered a chain reaction. The commotion reached the surveillance cameras, and within seconds, prison alarms blared as the Tactical Response Team rushed in.

"Down! Down! Down!" the aggressive guards yelled as they rushed into the cellblock.

We were ordered to lie down on the floor, a directive that inmates dared not defy, as the guards swiftly used batons and mace to subdue anyone who resisted.

While I lay on the floor, I could see Maurice a few feet away, handcuffed by the furious correctional officers. The incident had been captured in real time on their monitors, leaving no doubt about the culprit. A redneck guard began to approach Maurice, taunting him, "You want to throw televisions, boy? We've got a nice place for you, boy! Let's go!"

Maurice was dragged away and placed in the isolation unit on twenty-three-hour lockdown. He would spend the rest of his time there in a single-man cell, with only one hour a day for showering and minimal exercise in a cramped recreation area. It was a harsh consequence for his impulsive act of destroying a television, paid for by Virginia taxpayers. Maurice was playing a dangerous game because being sent to the isolation unit was not something to take lightly. Now he would be locked in a concrete box where he could only argue with himself.

In some facilities, an inmate locked away in isolation may not see another human being for days, weeks, or months. In extreme cases, he can be restricted from having any contact with humans for years. In the isolation unit, meals are delivered through a small slot in the steel prison cell door. An inmate's mental state may take a beating, and he can be damaged for life. After just a week in what may feel like psychological darkness, he may begin to have suicidal thoughts. The pressure is enormous, and the walls may seem to close in around the unwitting prisoner who often has no true understanding of what's happening to him. He may start to hallucinate or randomly count miscellaneous things. He may find himself counting the sound of each footstep the guard takes, as he walks down the long hallway, passing by his cell. He may begin to count the cracks in the wall, the ceiling, and the floor inside his cell. Or he may count droplets of water as they slowly drip out of the faucet. At one point, a man might count fifty thousand drops of water, for recreation, as they float down and splash ominously into the steel sink. After a while, the sound becomes overwhelming to his ears and that is when he may realize that he's in trouble in there.

For most of the day, inmates in the general population were confined to their housing units, with plenty of idle time to think about their past mistakes. Thoughts of what could have been or what went wrong often haunted them, making it a challenging mental battle.

A few weeks later, I received news from home that my former girlfriend was expecting a child with her new boyfriend. We hadn't been together for years, and we hadn't spoken in a long time, but the news was still hard to digest. I needed to focus on mentally preparing for my impending transfer to a federal penitentiary. Although I was not in love with this woman, I still cared for her, and it was tough to hear the news like that.

Ironically, I had watched other prisoners go through similar situations with wives, girlfriends, and even mistresses. To learn something like that over the phone while incarcerated was a hard pill to swallow, but even getting the information in person, in a prison visiting room, was tough too. You might also get the "I'm moving on," message sealed in an envelope and delivered by the US Postal Service. There are a lot of things that happen on the outside that an inmate has no control over. The world does not stop just because you're in prison. From breakups to divorces and betrayal, I've heard it all and I have seen it all. I have heard the threats being made over the phone to the former lover who they believe has wronged them. I've heard guys threatening to commit suicide over the indiscretions of their significate other. I've also seen inmates placed on psychiatric medication, because prison staff were concerned they would harm themselves. And yet, despite knowing all of that, never in a million years did I see something like this coming my way. But I should have. Sometimes the truth hurts, but very few men living the street life think about their girlfriend or ex-girlfriend moving on if they land behind bars. Most of the time, it is the last thing on their minds. I was jolted by the news, but regardless, I still had to serve the time I was sentenced to serve by a federal judge. How was I supposed to react? Was I supposed to toss the television on the floor and get thrown in the isolation unit, or was I supposed to take it like a man?

I was lying in my bunk thinking about the situation when Damion walked over to me. I think he may have noticed that something was wrong.

"What's going on, bro?" he asked.

"I'm good, man. Getting some rest."

"You good?"

"I got some crazy news today. My ex is having a kid with some dude, but it is what it is."

"That's crazy! I hope nothing like that happens while I'm here. I would kill my daughter's mother."

"That ain't me, bro. I ain't down with that. We weren't together when I got arrested, so she don't have no obligation to me." I said.

"I'm just saying. My daughter's mother knows not to mess with me like that."

"Were y'all together when you got arrested?" I said.

"No. I had a lot of girls when I caught this case. She knew that."

Quickly I realized that this conversation with Damion was not going anywhere. We had two totally different belief systems when it came to this issue. And as it turned out, his attitude towards relationships would later come back to cause him an enormous amount of legal trouble and grief.

"But you think she shouldn't move on while you're in jail, even though you were doing your thing out there?"

"Like I said, she know better," he said.

Even though he sounded irrational, I was not surprised by his comments. In fact, I heard similar statements from other guys, and the more I heard them, the more I began to understand how illogical they were. No woman is compelled to sit around waiting for a guy who is in prison, especially if he was not loyal to her before his legal troubles began. Loyalty is a two-way street, but I guess Damion did not see it that way.

In February 2003, it was time for me to be transferred from Virginia to a federal prison to begin serving my ninety-two-month sentence. My environment was about to change drastically, as I would be moving to a maximum-security prison with inmates serving long sentences. Many of them had nothing to lose, and an outburst like smashing a television could lead to severe consequences.

Early one morning, a prison guard woke me up and informed me of my imminent transfer. I was to pack my personal belongings and prepare for the move. In the Intake and Reception area, I joined thirty other inmates awaiting various destinations—some going to court, some heading home, and others uncertain of their next stop. To my surprise, John Allen Muhammad and Lee Boyd Malvo, the DC Sniper suspects, were also among the inmates in the holding cell, despite their high-profile status.

Muhammad acknowledged me with a simple, "What's up, my brother."

I replied, "Not much. How you holding up?"

"I can't complain," he said.

"Complaining ain't gonna change a thing, right?" I said.

Muhammad's demeanor had shifted from the cheerful and relaxed person I had previously seen. He and John Allen both seemed perplexed and lost in thought. I couldn't help but wonder what led them to embark on such a bizarre and senseless journey. More details of their motives had surfaced in the media, raising questions about their mental state and rationality. That's when I came to the conclusion that there some people who struggle with their mental health so much, the only choices they are capable of making are bad ones.

# CHAPTER 2
# BEHIND THE FENCE

*Winter 2003*
*Federal Correctional Institute Allenwood*
*Allentown, Pennsylvania*

THE TENSION INSIDE THE ALLENWOOD Federal Correctional Institute, located high up in the mountains of Central Pennsylvania, was electrifying. The prison was filled with gangsters, drug smugglers, serial killers, terrorists, and every street gang or sociopath one could imagine. The pressure there was piercing, and everyone could feel it. This is just one of the 122 prison facilities within the United States Federal Prison System which include prison camps and supermax penitentiaries where some inmates are housed in underground concrete bunkers. For me it was a simple proposition: mind your business, serve your time, and don't get too comfortable with the people around you.

The prisoner housing units at Allenwood Federal Correctional Institute were isolated from the rest of the prison compound by a formidable barbed-wire fence. On the other side of this fence lay the education building, the recreation yard, the dining facility, administrative offices, and the prison infirmary. Access to this area required inmates to pass through a secure checkpoint equipped with metal detectors. These precautions were implemented by the prison administration due to the frequent occurrence of violent assaults involving knives. This checkpoint was commonly referred to as the "gatehouse," and passing through it was the only way to reach the other side of the compound. I would traverse the gatehouse six to eight times a day, either to get to the education building, cafeteria, or to access the recreation yard.

One morning, the prison was on administrative lockdown due to heavy snowfall, causing the guards to be delayed in unlocking the cells. Around 11:00 a.m., an officer assigned to Housing Unit D began walking up the cellblock steps, making a loud jingling noise with his keys. He then proceeded to shout orders to the 224 inmates confined in their eight-foot-by-ten-foot prison cells.

"Prepare to unlock! Unlock in ten minutes!" the guard yelled out.

Then, he focused his attention on a short-statured inmate named Guapo, who happened to be the only inmate outside of his cell at that moment mopping the floor.

"Hey, you! Finish up and get back to your cell; unlock time in ten minutes," the guard instructed.

However, Guapo was not your typical janitor. He held a high-ranking position in a prison gang and had considerable influence over the dynamics inside the facility.

"Okay, no problem, boss. *No hay problema, jefe*," Guapo responded, acknowledging the guard's directive. He pushed his mop bucket toward the utility closet for storage and began walking down the tier, passing by the locked cells to his right. As he walked by, he observed Hispanic inmates inside their cells taping layers of reading magazines to their torsos, a tactic employed to protect their midsections during knife fights. It was something akin to wearing a makeshift bulletproof vest. Further down the tier, Guapo saw other gang members sharpening makeshift weapons and preparing for a potential conflict.

Inside this barbaric environment, creativity becomes an oxymoron, and the dark side is not far away. So, as Guapo continued to walk down the tier, the scenery became even more disturbing. As he walked by another cell, he could see another one of his brothers inside preparing for battle by inserting a shank wrapped in plastic up his anal cavity. It was his desperate attempt to conceal a weapon from the guards and deceive the metal detectors inside the gatehouse. Although the guards occasionally conducted cavity searches, they were rare, and everyone knew it.

Moments later, the guard returned to the cellblock, announcing, "Unlock time! The compound is open!" He manually unlocked all fifty-six cell doors on the lower level, one by one, repeating, "The compound is now open!"

As inmates exited their cells and moved into the common area for activities like watching television, taking showers, or using the inmate telephones, I watched from my cell-door window. It was then that I saw a Cuban inmate passing by, and I couldn't help but notice a sense of fear in his eyes. Something was clearly wrong.

My cellmate, Sal, an Italian mobster from Brooklyn, began to share a rumor he had heard during his time in the prison infirmary.

"I know you like to jog around the rec yard with your earphones on, but be careful today, young fella," Sal cautioned me. "These guys are dangerous." According to Sal, a contract was put out on another inmate by Hispanic gang members, and everyone had been warned to be vigilant. Being in the wrong place at the wrong time could have dire consequences. "I've already told my people to keep their distance," Sal added.

I paid close attention to Sal's concerns, but I had witnessed similar scenarios on multiple occasions in the past.

Years earlier, I had experienced a prison riot in a California state prison, involving a hundred Mexican inmates brawling in the recreation yard. I had also survived a serious altercation in FCI Petersburg, where inmates from Washington, DC, had clashed with fifty prisoners armed with knives from Cleveland.

"I heard the rumor, Sal," I responded. "Some Muslim brothers were talking about it in the law library. But I'm not worried. As long as they clear the snow from the track, I plan to get some laps in."

Running was my way of maintaining some normalcy within the prison walls. I was no stranger to the harsh prison environment, and I knew how to navigate it. In such an environment, you had to be prepared for bad things to happen every day and adapt.

As inmates began to leave the housing unit and walked down the partially shoveled sidewalk towards the gatehouse, it was evident that tensions were running high. No one was talking, and everyone was vigilant, watching their surroundings closely. Allenwood's most dangerous inmates, identifiable by tattoos depicting violent imagery, were prepared for a confrontation. I had my running shoes on and kept a safe distance from the crowd while wearing headphones with the volume lowered, maintaining a watchful eye on the situation.

The leader of the group planning the attack was an inmate named Juan Carlos, a seasoned Colombian assassin with a stocky build who wore an eye patch. Rumor had it that he had taken a bullet to the head in Miami while involved in cocaine trafficking for the Cali Cartel. In Allenwood, Juan Carlos held a position as an enforcer for the Colombian inmates, and significant decisions within their group required his approval.

As inmates passed through the gatehouse and metal detectors, an eerie silence prevailed, and you could hear a pin drop. Just on the other side of the gatehouse, in the heart of the prison compound, Guapo initiated his assault, and his victim never saw it coming.

"Stick him!" the assailants shouted.

The Cuban inmate tried to defend himself, but Guapo's homemade knife found its mark, piercing his lung. As he stumbled through the snow, the Cuban was relentlessly attacked by Juan Carlos and others involved in the brawl. Bright red blood spurted from his wounds like a malfunctioning water fountain, and he cried out in agony. The hit squad was efficient, and the Cuban was left battered but still standing. "*Cortar a la perra otra vez*," the assassins roared, signaling for the attack to continue. The Cuban fell to the ground like a felled tree, and that fast it was over.

I couldn't help but mutter to myself, "Damn, they got him."

One of the several video surveillance cameras positioned around the prison compound captured the altercation, and as the loud prison siren blared, members of the Tactical Response Team rushed towards the scene.

Dressed in black fatigues and combat armor, they resembled soldiers prepared for combat. Some of the guards were known for their aggression, not hesitating to use their batons to strike inmates. "Down, down, down!" they yelled as scores of inmates spread-eagled on the ground. However, by the time they arrived, the Cuban lay in a pool of red snow, and his attackers had fled.

Minutes later, the injured Cuban was carried away on a stretcher and transported to a local hospital where he recovered from his wounds. This was the harsh reality of life behind bars, a world where violence was sometimes inflicted by sociopaths or individuals with serious mental health issues that fueled aggression. It was an environment where violence was often the default method for settling disputes and could escalate fast.

Shortly afterward, details of the premeditated attack began to emerge. Word around the prison compound suggested that the Cuban had been mutilated due to a drug transaction gone wrong. Allegedly, cocaine had been smuggled into the prison's visiting room by a family member of one of the Colombian inmates. The Cuban was supposed to take possession of the contraband and transport it back to the inmate housing unit. Once secured inside the unit, the drugs were to be handed over to the Colombians for distribution to other prisoners. Inside the prison, cocaine was a valuable commodity, and everyone, including the Cuban, knew it, which may have motivated him to steal half of the illicit substance for himself.

Immediately after the attack, inmates were ordered to return to their cells, and the entire facility was placed on lockdown—a measure used by prison administrators as both punishment and a way to prevent retaliation among prisoners after an incident. All inmates were confined to their cells indefinitely, with only one hour allowed outside for showers. Fortunately, I had at least two months' worth of books to keep me occupied, so to me, it was just another day in the neighborhood.

As I made my way back to the housing unit, I casually remarked to one of the guards, "I guess we'll be on lockdown for a while?"

His response was grim: "Yeah...welcome to hell."

# CHAPTER 3

# WELCOME TO THE YARD

A FEW MONTHS AFTER THE Cuban was viciously assaulted and butchered on the compound, the brutal winter weather in Central Pennsylvania had evolved into the beauty of spring. Sometimes I would stand in the middle of the recreation yard, gazing past the fence, admiring the lush green mountaintops that surrounded the prison. The views were breathtaking, and the tall trees lining the palisades provided a sense of tranquility. I would linger there, on the inside of the sharp razor wire, imagining what life would be like on the other side. Although the picturesque scenery was soothing and enticing at that moment, for the next few years, it would remain beyond my reach.

I began experiencing vivid dreams almost every night, dreams of being released from prison and returning home. However, these dreams always took a dark turn as demons would suddenly appear and block my path at the front gate, preventing my release. These dreams began optimistically but always ended in disappointment. I used to interpret them as a message from some higher power, a warning to leave the illegal drug trade behind or face a lifetime in prison. That was how I interpreted it at the time. The truth was, I no longer had an appetite for fast money and fast cars. I had nothing left to prove except staying alive in prison long enough to reunite with my children. I wanted no part of that world, but before I could return to my family, I had to make it out of Allenwood alive.

One day, I was leaving the recreation yard after spending several hours working out and headed back to the housing unit. Somedays I would run for miles around the track, until I was completely exhausted, just to combat the insomnia I was having. Being completely exhausted was the only way I could sleep at night. That's when I spotted a group of "new fish" walking across the compound. These newly arriving inmates were being escorted by two prison staff members to the housing units where they would be living for the next two, five, or thirty years: it all depends. You could tell they had just arrived simply by the look on their faces. Many of them were disheveled and in a daze wondering how the hell they got to this strange place high up in the mountains. They were sizing up their new unfamiliar environment while, at the same time, their unfamiliar environment was sizing them up as well.

Among them, walking in the midst of the group, was Damion "Soul" Neal, the guy I had been with in Virginia a few months earlier. As we reached the front door of Housing Unit D, I greeted him, "Yo, what's up, man?"

It took him a moment to recognize me. I had gained some healthy weight and shaved, making me look quite different from the desperado he had met in Northern Neck Regional.

"What's up, bro? How long you been here?" he asked.

"A few months. After I left Virginia, they sent me back to Baltimore for a few days, then a prison bus picked up about twenty of us. We stopped in Lewisburg and ended up here."

"How's this place?" Damion inquired.

"It's alright."

"I got here three hours ago. Been sitting over in Intake, filling out paperwork since this morning."

"You need anything?" I offered.

"A toothbrush and some soap, for sure. I won't have any money in my account for a few days."

"I'll be right back," I assured him.

When a new inmate arrives at a facility, they're momentarily lost, needing time to adjust to their new home. Compared to other inmates, Damion had relatively little time left on his sentence before his scheduled release—about a year if he stayed out of trouble. Calling a year remaining on a sentence "short time" might sound odd, but there were inmates in Allenwood serving sentences spanning decades—forty, fifty, or even sixty years. They had little to look forward to and no plans to reunite with their families anytime soon. Their futures appeared bleak, and the stress of serving such lengthy sentences without hope can feel like psychological torture, drowning the mind in despair.

A few weeks after Damion's arrival, he asked the guard to move him from his initially assigned cell to the one on the upper tier, where I resided. Sal had moved downstairs with one of his Italian buddies, leaving an empty bunk in my cell. Sharing a cell with someone you got along with always made prison life a bit easier.

Once Damion settled in, we often discussed the street culture that had ensnared so many lives. Those involved in the street life typically knew one another or had connections to the same people. In our case, we knew many of the same individuals. We would talk late into the night about bizarre moments, like the time Joe Green ran from the police, leapt off a roof, and landed on the hood of a police car. Joe survived the fall but still ended up in prison. Rumor had it that he was running from both his girlfriend and the cops simultaneously, making that day a part of street folklore.

"You got a kid, right?" I asked Damion.

"Yeah, a daughter," he replied.

"How old is she?"

"Eight."

"Wow, she's young, bro."

"Yeah, it's been tough. She doesn't like coming to jails to visit."

"Leaving a child without their father is tough, especially if you care about them. Leaving a daughter out there, unable to protect her, is even harder," I mused.

Among the inmates in Allenwood from Baltimore were individuals serving time for various crimes, including drug distribution, handgun violations, and even bank robbery. Some had committed kidnapping and other violent offenses. Most of them kept a low profile, aiming to serve their time with minimal stress and return to the streets.

The United States accounts for just 5 percent of the world's population, yet it comprises 25 percent of the world's prison population. The inside of a federal prison is one of the most segregated places in America, and this point is magnified significantly inside the cafeteria. White inmates sat on one side of the cafeteria, while Latino and Hispanic inmates congregated in the middle. On the opposite end of the mess hall the largest demographic in federal prison was located: African American men. To the naked eye, the cafeteria resembled the borders of different countries separated by varying skin colors.

Most of the guys from Baltimore sat together in the cafeteria, building camaraderie, or just passing the time. We gossiped about the latest federal indictments hitting the city, who was headed to the penitentiary for the next twenty years, and who had a contract out on whom. But we also joked around a lot. We had nothing but time on our hands, and sometimes we had to manufacture laughter just to make it through the day, the month, or the year.

"Man, this food is garbage. They would never serve this in Lewisburg. Guys at the Burg would riot." Those were the colorful words spewed out by a Jamaican inmate from

Baltimore named Dennis Belafonte. Some of the guys called him Belafonte, while others simply called him Bell. He was serving time for heroin distribution and racketeering and had been behind the fence for eighteen straight years. He was funny at times and loved to gamble, mostly on college and professional football games. Gambling was the vice he used to stay sane while giving more than a decade and a half of his life to the Federal Bureau of Prisons. He ran a small gambling operation right there in Allenwood, which was a thorn in the side of some prison officials. Although it was illegal, as long as it didn't stir up any tension in the prison, most of the staff looked the other way.

"You eat any more of this crap, you might die. This ain't right." Those were the remarks made by Gee, another inmate from Baltimore. Gee was a career criminal and a veteran of prison life. His original criminal case was bank robbery, but when I met him, he was in jail because of his tenth parole violation. He was preparing to be released in less than a year, and he had no problem reminding everyone of that.

"I'm going home soon, and I won't have to deal with this. I'm going home."

"We know you're going home, Gee! You talk about it every goddamn day!" Belafonte said.

Gee was older than most of us, but sometimes he had the mental ability of a teenager. Some of the things he would say would leave everyone scratching their heads and trying desperately to understand him.

"Yo, Bell! You right, man. I'm not eating this shit. This is crazy." That was Eric B, another inmate from Baltimore serving seven years for conspiracy to distribute crack cocaine. Eric B got along with almost everyone. When he was on the street, he was a ladies' man, and now he just wanted to do his time and go home. He was trying hard to stay out of trouble because he wanted to be released on time, and not a day later.

He did not want anything to do with any matter that could result in him losing good-time credits and extending his stay in Allenwood. Good-time credits were a valuable commodity that most guys did not want to lose over disciplinary issues. With good-time credits, you got out of prison on your original release date, but without them, you simply stayed a little longer.

We were all eating lunch in the cafeteria when Gee dropped another bombshell. He had a habit of making pronouncements in the mess hall, but even for his standards, this one was huge.

"I'm gonna get married before I leave."

This caught everyone by surprise.

"You've got less than a year left. Why the hell you want to do something like that? You're going to be stuck with that gold-digger when you get out," Belafonte said.

The guys around the table began to laugh.

"She ain't no gold-digger, Bell."

Gee's feelings were bruised by the harsh remarks, but I didn't think Bell was trying to be disrespectful. I think he was just trying to make a point and maybe have a little fun, I guess.

"Alright, man, alright!" Belafonte said with a smile. "I'm just joking. You only have a few months to go before you hit the street, right?"

"Yeah."

"So, why don't you just wait until you go home and then get married? How long have you known this *bumbaclot*?"

Uncontrollable laughter ensued.

"That ain't funny, Bell!" Gee said. "I met her two months ago. My cousin introduced me to her on the phone."

"And you want to marry her already? Come on, man!" Eric B said.

The rest of us were trying to hold in our laughter, but we couldn't, and soon the conversation became a big spectacle.

Each month, on designated days, wedding ceremonies were performed inside the prison visiting room by the prison chaplain. Several prisoners married for love, and some even married for access to a green card. Then there were those who were running an even more elaborate scam on their prospective brides. What was Gee's motivation for wanting to get married in Allenwood? I had no idea.

"Man, all those women out on the street, and you want to get married here? You crazy!" Eric B said.

I was trying to stay out of it, but it was not easy. At this point, we were just having fun, but all at Gee's expense.

"Come on, man, stop playing. You talking about the girl in the picture you showed me?" Damion said.

"What's wrong with her?" Belafonte asked.

And that's when I couldn't resist. "Come on, Gee? What you doing, man?" I said.

"Man, fuck y'all!" Gee said. Then, he stood up from the table, stormed out of the cafeteria, and everyone laughed. As usual, Belafonte was the instigator, and at times, he could be a real comedian. Gee had this way about himself where it was hard to take him seriously, no matter what the topic of discussion was about.

Most of these guys were casualties of the War on Drugs and now were part of the dysfunctional world of incarceration. It felt good sometimes to joke around with the guys I had built rapport with over time. In a strange way, it was like a brotherhood. But at the end of the day, I knew where I was, and I couldn't afford to take this environment for granted. We were still in an unpredictable place where laughter could turn from a bright light into darkness in sixty seconds or less.

Early on, I realized that Damion was a smart guy, and he had a bright future awaiting him if he wanted it and if he was willing to make some changes in his life. Like all of us, he was rough around the edges, but I could see that he was capable of turning things around. If he wanted to do something besides hustling in the streets, he had the tools needed to do so. It was clear he could accomplish whatever he wanted if he set his mind to it.

Late one night—a night I remember well—the housing unit was dead silent. Damion and I were sitting in our cell, talking about a host of different subjects. It was at that moment when I got a closer look at who he was as a human being. He had removed the mask, if only for a minute or two.

"What's your plan when you get out?" I asked.

"There's a lot I want to do, but I know I have to stay out there to do them."

"Have you signed up for any education programs?"

"Not yet, but I'm going to. I need a good job when I get out of here so I can take care of my daughter."

"I feel you, bro," I said.

"This jail shit gets old after a while. We're sitting here wasting away like old vegetables. Life ain't waiting for nobody."

"You got that right," I said.

"Nothing stands still out there. The only thing standing still is us, waiting to be fed, waiting to take a shower, and waiting to take a shit. Ain't no progress in here."

"So, what's the plan, because without a plan everything else is just talk," I said.

"I've been thinking about moving to Atlanta. I want to get back into music. I want to get back to doing things I like. I like music," said Damion.

"So, you trying to be Jay-Z?"

We both laughed.

There were times when Damion was focused on doing the things he needed to do behind the fence to turn his world around. I would see him doing a lot of reading and studying. You did not have to be a genius to understand that street life was not working out so well for him. And you did not have to be a genius to understand that the penitentiary is not a fulfilling place to be or a place that will satisfy a man with the least bit of ambition.

"Atlanta might be a good place for you," I said. "A lot of people are moving down south. Sometimes you need a change of scenery. You don't want to be one of the guys sitting here with fifty years or a life sentence."

"I heard the guy upstairs from New York got sixty years," Damion said.

"You talking about Ace?" I said.

"Yeah."

"His cell buddy got one hundred years for selling crack," I said.

"I don't know what I would do with a prison sentence that long. I might kill myself," Damion said.

I laughed and said, "Man, you wouldn't kill yourself. You would just do the time and deal with it the best way you could."

"Seriously. I would kill myself if I had that much time," he said. "What's a man gonna do in prison that long?"

I could see that Damion was serious when he made that statement. We were there in the cell alone, and he was being candid. I could see it in his eyes, and I could hear it in his voice that he meant every word. Spending that much time in prison was a painful proposition for him to contemplate. Seeing inmates who you had built rapport with walking around with double- and triple-digit prison sentences was depressing. Even though that may not have been your reality, it's still jarring to the senses. But it could also be a wakeup call for you to get serious about your own journey and prepare for a future that doesn't include a criminal lifestyle.

"Honestly, if I had a fifty-year sentence, I wouldn't know what to do, either. That's why I am never gonna put myself in a situation like that," I said. "We act like some of this stuff happens by accident. Yeah, the system is screwed up, but we need to stop putting ourselves in harm's way. Stop jumping in front of the goddamn bullet."

Damion did not respond. He just sat there with his head down, staring at the floor.

"Come over to the education building tomorrow and hang out. They got all kinds of books over there. You can even study for your CDLs."

"Yeah, I need to take care of that," he said.

"You better do something soon, bro. You ain't got a lot of time left."

"I'm coming over tomorrow. Definitely," he said.

"This is probably the only opportunity in your life you'll have this much time to work on you. In the streets, you gonna be looking for a job and trying to put food on the table. If you don't do it now, you ain't never going to," I said.

"Yeah, you're right."

"I'm taking college classes in business, so I'll have something when I get out of here. I can't afford to go back to hustling," I said.

"I get it, bro. I get it. Plus, it's so many guys dying out there. Two years ago, my homie got killed right in front of me. Shit tore me apart."

"How? What happened?"

"We had beef with some guys from Biddle Street. One night we were at my friend Keith's house drinking in the living room. Our phones kept ringing, but we didn't answer. A few minutes later, somebody started shooting through the window."

"Damn."

"Everybody dove on the floor, but Keith got shot in the head. Later, we learned that his neighbor was calling us to say that a guy wearing a mask was standing outside the window, but we wouldn't answer."

I could see that Damion was still trying to cope with the trauma he'd experienced that night. At the time, I didn't understand how people were affected long-term by incidents like the ones he described, but I could see that it bothered him a lot.

"Blood was everywhere. We called 911, and the cops got there first, then the ambulance. They rushed him to Johns Hopkins Hospital, but he was brain dead." Damion paused and then said, "Seeing that really messed me up."

These kinds of stories are far too familiar in Baltimore. For many of the twenty-something-year-old Black males living there, growing old is not a term often used to describe their future. And if you're lucky enough to make it past twenty-five years old, you may feel like you made it, but you still may have been traumatized in some way and scarred for the rest of your life. You may even have mental baggage that goes unaddressed because you don't fully understand how you've been negatively affected.

"They killed my homeboy, and his grandmother had to see that. After that, it was all-out war."

"What happened next?" I asked.

"The girlfriend of one of the guys involved in the shooting was kidnapped, but before they let her go, they shot her in the neck. Then, the same guys who killed Keith got into a shootout on Lafayette Street, and a two-year-old was hit," he said.

I didn't know it at the time, but Damion was referring to a violent feud between two area street gangs that lasted for months. At the height of their murderous conflict, twelve people were shot and one died during a memorial service for Keith. Keith's mother was one of the people wounded that day. Damion was present for the service, and although he was not physically injured, he was traumatized in a way he had never been before.

"It was ugly, man. People were sprawled on the ground, bleeding," he said.

The woman who lost her life that day was the girlfriend of Damion's best friend. A bullet struck her in the head, and she was quickly transported to the hospital, where she was pronounced dead.

"I never thought they would stoop that low. It was the worst shit I had ever seen in my life," Damion lamented. "The feds indicted them for drugs and murder. They ain't never getting out of jail, man. Never."

# CHAPTER 4

# MY BROTHER'S KEEPER

ALLENWOOD FEDERAL PRISON WAS AN arduous place with layers upon layers of dysfunction at every turn. In late 2003, I was attending college courses four times a week. My major was Business Management, and I enjoyed getting an education that I knew would help me when I returned to society. I was well aware that a formal education was crucial to securing a decent job post-release, and I was fully committed. In the evenings, the same college professors who taught at the local community college came into the prison to conduct classes.

It was during my time at Allenwood, while taking these courses, that I began to take writing seriously. My English class demanded a substantial amount of writing, providing me with the opportunity to hone my storytelling skills. Back then, I enjoyed writing, but I never could have imagined how far that skill would take me. Allenwood was also where I enrolled in my first college-level public speaking course. Initially, I hated the class because I felt uneasy making formal presentations in front of fellow inmates. However, as the semester progressed, I grew more comfortable with myself.

Our education paralleled that of college students on the outside. We followed the same curriculum and received transferable credits, making it possible to apply to other colleges and universities upon release. Access to college courses within the prison system has become more prevalent, but it's important to note that not all inmates are interested in a college education, and some may opt for vocational training. The overall literacy rate among inmates is lower than the national average, which can discourage some from seeking a formal education. Some people frown on the idea that inmates have an opportunity to attend college while in prison, but the truth is over 90 percent of the men and women currently incarcerated will return to society someday. Given the right resources they can become productive citizens, but without the right resources many of them will continue to be a thorn in the side of the community.

One evening, while I sat at my small steel desk inside my cell, studying for an upcoming accounting exam, Damion suddenly burst through the cell door, trying to catch his breath.

"Yo, it's going down!" he exclaimed.

"What?" I said.

"It's Rock from Baltimore. He got beef with Guapo."

Damion had my full attention, but I still didn't fully grasp the situation.

"Rock got a knife. He's gonna stab Guapo in the gym tonight. He wants everybody to meet in the recreation yard to watch his back."

"Wait a minute! What happened?" I inquired.

"You remember Neko? The guy Rock had a thing with?"

"What about it?" I replied.

"Last year Guapo was dealing with Neko and now he wants them to get back together. Today, Guapo approached Rock and told him to stay away from him. Rock said he gonna cut Guapo ass up."

I started to feel anger welling up within me.

"You want to get involved in this soap-opera shit and you're only a few months away from getting out?" I asked.

Guapo and Rock were on the verge of committing assault or attempted murder inside a federal prison due to a dispute centered around a personal relationship with another inmate. They were ready to jeopardize their release over prison drama, and Damion wanted us to get entangled in it.

"Fuck that!" I exclaimed. "I'm not calling my mother to tell her I stabbed a guy and won't be home for another five years. Are you stupid?"

Damion was contemplating involvement in a situation that could severely harm his chances of reuniting with his daughter, whom he professed to love. I, on the other hand, had no intention of making such a reckless choice.

"Look, man," Damion argued, "Our homie is about to get it on. I can't leave him hanging."

"Then tell him to sit his clown ass down!" I retorted.

I had spent enough time behind bars to understand the unspoken rules governing alliances among inmates from the same cities or towns. They typically support each other in altercations, but there were exceptions, and this was one of them.

"Let me explain something. I don't follow behind stupid shit, okay. What I look like getting involved in that?"

I was annoyed with the conversation because it just didn't make sense. It didn't make sense that I had to explain this to another grown man.

"Two sodomites running around like savages, and you ready to die for them? You think they would do the same for you?" I asked.

While witnessing fellow inmates getting into serious trouble in prison was never a pleasant sight for me, especially when it was over nonsense, I wasn't about to compromise myself for something that made no sense.

"Listen, finish your time and go home. Be smart," I said.

And despite all the drama over the potential altercation between Rock and Guapo, the situation never escalated to violence. The two men discussed their "dispute" and decided to let it go. Guapo was planning to be released in nine months, and Rock was going home in less than two years. Their issues with one another, regardless of how strange they were, had the potential to drag other people down with them. They realized the tension they had amongst themselves was not worth jeopardizing their return to society, so they ended it before it got out of control.

Same-sex relationships in prison do occur, but contrary to what many people believe, they're rare and small in scope. It's a dangerous situation to get involved in while you're incarcerated. But, regardless of their sexual orientation, the situation that Guapo and Rock were involved in could have erupted badly. A prison environment is a powder keg where several inmates are dealing with all types of diagnosed and undiagnosed mental health disorders, some acute and some severe. Once you add a sexual relationship into that equation, it has the potential to explode, and if it does, look out.

And I know the media likes to glorify violence in prison and its brutality, but the truth is in twelve years, I've never seen an instance where an inmate forced his penis into another man. I'm not saying it never happens. What I'm saying is, rape in prison is rare, but that's not how the media depicts that environment.

In life, everyone must make choices about what matters to them and what doesn't, but these decisions are especially critical behind the fence. The stakes are high, and missteps can result in the loss of freedom or even life. It's easy to act recklessly during tense moments, but blindly leaping into situations is not the answer.

I consider myself an expert in one thing: survival in prison. It's something you learn along the way, and you learn it quickly. Witnessing individuals come dangerously close to losing their lives taught me the importance of making well-thought-out decisions for one's own survival.

The pressure of incarceration can be overwhelming, even for the toughest individuals. The burden of being confined behind steel and concrete walls for years is immense. Alongside the stress, there's a pervasive sense of insecurity and uncertainty. The constant threat of violence in prison can have a profound psychological impact, akin to the suffocating presence of old cigar smoke. It lingers in the air, serving as a constant reminder of its existence.

In the fall of 2003, the DC Sniper trial dominated the news on CNN and other national news networks. The case also made headlines in nearly every newspaper and was a frequent topic on syndicated radio talk shows across America. In November of that year, John Allen Muhammad stood trial for the murder of Dean Myers and was subsequently found guilty and sentenced to death. Information about this case was almost unavoidable, even within the confines of federal prison. I recall reading about their plans to shoot a pregnant woman in the stomach and their plot to kill a police officer, with the intention of detonating explosives at the officer's funeral to harm more law enforcement officials. It seemed like they had everything planned out until the day they got arrested.

# CHAPTER 5

# NOT ROSA PARKS

IN PRISON, THE FEELING OF winning any type of extra-curricular activity is magnified by leaps and bounds compared to normal society. Whether it's a simple game of cards or a chess match with another inmate, the emotions associated with both victory and defeat are intensified. Everything, from determining who can do the most pushups to who can run the fastest mile—they all hold significant importance. Each win soothes the ego of the incarcerated individual, while every loss crushes it.

At Allenwood, watching professional sports on television was akin to the Holy Grail of television programming. While most avid sports fans are passionate about their favorite teams' success or failure, for someone in prison, these emotions are multiplied a millionfold. Sports became our stress reliever, occasionally even a stress multiplier, serving as a temporary escape until the next World Series, Super Bowl, or National Championship. It was one of the few activities that helped us endure the day, month, or even the decade.

In Allenwood, men watched golf superstar Tiger Woods play in tournaments with the same enthusiasm as if they were watching Beyoncé and Jay-Z live in concert. For them, watching Tiger was like any other championship event. Despite most of them never having set foot on a golf course, they cheered and yelled at the television every time Tiger sank a putt.

"Hell yeah, that's right, Tiger!"

"That's what I'm talking about!"

Before Woods became a professional golfer, these men had never paid much attention to golf. And it was the first time I had ever seen Black men so excited about the game. In Allenwood, and in our minds, Tiger Woods was one of us, or at least pretty darn close.

For men who didn't have much else to cheer about, sports meant everything. Their wives and girlfriends had left them, their kids no longer wanted to visit, and their lives had been turned upside down by federal law enforcement officials. Michael Jordan, Mike Tyson, or even Olympic sprinter Michael Johnson were the only family they had left, in their minds. It provided them with something to look forward to during a time when most of them had nothing.

One evening, the New York Knicks, an NBA basketball team, was playing against the Los Angeles Lakers at the famous Madison Square Garden, with the game televised nationwide. Approximately fifty inmates were glued to the television, eager to witness the live action on the TNT network. It was trash-talking Kobe Bryant shooting jumpers from half court against the Knicks legend Patrick Ewing. New York fans sat on one side of the housing unit in chairs, while Los Angeles fans occupied the opposite side. It felt like being inside the Garden, though not quite. The scent of hot buttered popcorn cooking in the prison microwave oven hung in the air, and someone was passing around a large bag of Reese's Pieces purchased at the prison commissary. It was game night!

I had been a Knicks fan for years, so win or lose, I remained a diehard supporter. My fandom had begun when I bought tickets from scalpers on 7th Avenue in Manhattan when I was about twenty years old. The game started on time, and so did the trash talk. The housing unit came alive that night and guys were at the pinnacle of their rude and obnoxious behavior.

"Fuck the Knicks. They're garbage."

"Yo, Ace! You hear what this clown said? You better come check his ass."

"I heard his ass!" said Ace.

These were the moments I looked forward to, and that night, I laughed harder than I had in a long time. It was a moment to forget about everything else going on in our lives and simply enjoy the evening. Everyone has their "thing" to help them through tough times, and for us, watching professional sports on television was ours.

As the two NBA giants clashed that night, we watched and cheered. Even the television announcers couldn't hide their bias.

"Did you see that shot from Kobe?" one announcer exclaimed.

"Yeah, best player in the league," replied the other announcer. "He's amazing."

Even the elderly inmates, who typically watched conservative programming like National Geographic and Discovery Channel, couldn't help but pay attention to the game that night. It wasn't Shark Week, but it was still exciting and kept them on the edge of their seats.

Damion, an ardent Los Angeles Lakers fan, harbored a passionate hatred for New York. "Fuck the Knicks. The whole city is trash," he said.

Over the years, I had witnessed inmates exchange veiled personal insults while watching sporting events on television, and sometimes, it escalated into physical altercations. However, when it reached that level, it wasn't merely a basketball game that triggered someone's inclination for violence. It was often something deeper, like pent-up resentment, toxic masculinity, or hidden aggression that surfaced during these interactions.

Damion and a charismatic inmate from New York named Squirrel were sitting a few feet away from me, watching the game and engaging in a loud conversation that everyone could hear. Squirrel had been in prison for nearly a decade, serving a lengthy sentence for crack cocaine distribution. He was a boisterous character, standing at only five feet tall, and one of the loudest inmates in the housing unit. He was also an intelligent individual who I attended college courses with in the evenings.

"You don't understand. The Civil Rights Movement changed the course of this country," Squirrel said.

"Civil Rights ain't changed a damn thing. All that marching, and for what? We still ain't free," Damion said.

"What you don't understand is it wasn't just marching, and it wasn't just Doctor King or Rosa Parks. A lot of people got arrested for not getting out of their seat on the bus; she just became the most well-known. Do your fucking research."

While everyone else was watching basketball, for some reason, these two were debating the plight of American Civil Rights. I had no idea how their conversation shifted from Kobe Bryant to Rosa Parks, but nonetheless, they were fully engaged in their discussion.

"Hell with Rosa Parks!" Damion said loudly. "What she ever done for me? And screw that Civil Rights bullshit. Black people still screwed up! Ain't nothing changed!"

"You don't know what the fuck you're talking about!" Squirrel said. "We couldn't even drink out of the same goddamn water fountain as white folks, fool."

"Instead of slavery, we got jails. It's the same lies, under a different name. We still getting screwed by the same people that gave you Rosa Parks, King, and all that freedom garbage. The same people who created the hood, crack, and AIDS."

When Damion first arrived in Allenwood, he joined a religious organization named the Moorish Science Temple of America. They had a very "unique" ideology about America and the rest of the world, and they had unique opinions about how a Black man should conduct himself. In Allenwood, about thirty inmates belonged to the organization, enough to be widely recognized. You also knew that almost any conversation with them about race, Civil Rights, or the government would become intense. Damion strongly believed in the teachings and ideology of that organization, so his opinions and views on the Civil Rights Movement were not a surprise to me. Nevertheless, I was surprised by the level of disrespect he displayed towards iconic Civil Rights activists, and now he had generated a small audience.

"That Rosa Parks thing was a media stunt. It wasn't real. King was working for the feds, and so was she," he said.

"You sound dumb!" Squirrel retorted. "Yo, Kevin! Come get your crazy-ass homeboy. He losing his goddamn mind."

I heard Squirrel's statement, but I had no intention of getting involved in their conversation. In fact, I was doing my best to ignore them both and watch the basketball game, which was actually very good.

"Kev know what I'm saying is true," Damion said. "That's why he don't want to say nothing. He knows all this prison shit is just legalized kidnapping organized by the US government."

"I'm watching the game, bro. I'm not trying to get into that," I said.

"That's because you know the truth. You know Rosa Parks was a spy," he said.

And that's when he baited me in.

"Really, bro? You sound crazy right now," I said.

"Look around you. This ain't nothing but modern-day slavery. And yeah, Rosa Parks was a fraud!"

Damion was getting under my skin, and I believed at the time that he knew exactly what he was doing. I was trying to stay out of his conversation with Squirrel, but he was trying his best to pull me into their debate. I wasn't exactly what you would call a history buff, but I knew that Rosa Parks did a lot more for America than Damion and I ever had.

"What have you done to help Black folks? You were out in the street selling crack, right? Now you want to disrespect people who tried to do good when you haven't done good for nobody, not even for yourself," I said.

Then the guard appeared in the housing unit and announced that it was time for lockdown.

"Lockdown, lockdown," the guard yelled.

The ten o'clock institution-wide count was getting ready to begin soon, and all inmates were to report back to their cells. Within three minutes or so, all the prisoners who were watching the basketball game began to return to their cells, and the guard began locking the cell doors behind them.

Once we were locked inside our cells, the conversation between Damion and me intensified, and it got very loud. I was bothered by both his comments and by being dragged into his foolish debate. In my view, it seemed as if he was show-boating for the small audience of inmates who were listening to his conversation. That was how I interpreted that moment.

"You ain't no gangster, man, so stop with the bullshit," I said. Now it was my chance to get a few verbal jabs in, and I took advantage of the opportunity.

"You got a punk-ass gun case, so stop putting on a show for these motherfuckers. You ain't even knowledgeable enough about history to talk that Revolution shit."

"Fuck you," he said.

"Fuck you, too! What have you done for your people?" Damion did not respond. "That's what I thought!" I said.

I don't know why I took it so personally, but later that night, I realized something that changed my perspective. I realized that I may have wanted him to change and succeed more than he wanted to. I needed to focus on what Kevin Shird needed to do to advance his life when he got out of prison. I wasn't "fixed," and I didn't have all the answers. If I was so smart, why was I incarcerated, too? I was a work in progress, and I also knew that I had a lot more work to do.

The next morning, I left the housing unit early and went over to the recreation yard to run a few laps around the track. I had not slept well, but I figured I would get some rest later in the day. I had begun to have bad dreams again, and they were not your run-of-the-mill bad dreams either; they were more like gruesome nightmares.

Officials in Allenwood had no problem issuing an unlimited amount of sleeping pills and psychiatric medication to inmates. They preferred to have listless, laid-back, even lethargic inmates walking around the prison rather than men who were always on edge, or men who were on the verge of losing it and could harm someone, including a prison guard or staff member. Don't get me wrong; several inmates had valid reasons for taking sleep aids or psychiatric medication, but the process the administration had in place to evaluate inmates in need was easy to manipulate. I often wondered how many guys really should have been on medication and how many were just working the system. I thought seriously about getting sleeping pills to help me sleep at night, but I decided not to. For one thing, I hated taking pills of any kind, and secondly, I did not want to be dependent on a substance that could later become habitual. I was well aware of how easily a person could get addicted to a drug, and I didn't want anything to do with that. Also, I didn't think that pills were the answer to the question as to why I was still having these crazy nightmares after so many years. When I was in prison in

California and I would have a tough time sleeping, I would go out to the yard and run three miles every day just to sleep. At Allenwood, I began that same routine, and it served me well, but it still wasn't a cure for my problem.

Behind the fence, there's a lot of noise around you; noise meaning distractions. Everyone has personal baggage that they're trying to manage. If you can figure out how to block out the noise around you, at least you give yourself a chance. But if you're constantly consumed with someone else's mess, how are you going to have the energy to tend to your own problems?

Running was my way of easing the anxiety of being incarcerated. With every lap I ran past the guard tower, my energy was boosted, and something within me was reignited. When you're not conscious of the stress inside you, that's when it takes over you, and that's when you can become your own worst enemy. I had problems too, and I needed to make sure I had my own act together. It's easy to have all the answers for someone else's life, but you better make sure your own affairs are in order. I wouldn't be in prison forever. What was I going to do with the rest of my life when I returned to the streets? That was the matter I should have been focused on and not this other mess.

A few days after our dust-up over Rosa Parks and the American Civil Rights Movement, Damion seemed to refocus his priorities. I was working in the education building, and I would see him there checking out books from the library. He seemed excited about reading and gaining knowledge that could help him down the road. It really looked like he had turned the corner.

Damion worked in the prison kitchen and was assigned to the maintenance division, which handled repairing things like broken refrigerators, ovens, and damaged water pipes. Belafonte worked in the kitchen too, and they spoke often.

Bell was older than Damion, so he too offered him advice when the opportunity presented itself. The fact that they both were from East Baltimore gave them a lot to discuss. But they also talked about things that were going on around Allenwood, where Bell provided his blunt analysis.

"Me and your boy got into an argument the other day," Damion said.

"You always arguing with somebody. What happened this time?"

"Over Rosa Parks. He started talking trash, and we got into it. You know how I am."

"I know he didn't like that."

"I don't even care anymore. That dude thinks he knows everything."

"How the hell you start talking about Rosa Parks, anyway? I thought you were watching the Knicks?"

"You know him. I don't care what the conversation is about; he thinks he knows everything."

Belafonte laughed. "He does think he know everything sometimes, but that's my man. At the end of the day, he just wants everybody to be alright. Plus, he ain't no dummy, young fella. He was making a lot of money out in the streets. I know some of his people."

"All I'm saying is he gets on my damn nerves sometimes. Trust me, bro, I live in the cell with that nigga. I know what he was doing in the street, but I ain't no sucker."

"You're going home soon, right?" Bell said.

"Yeah."

"When?"

"In a couple more months."

"What are you going to do when you get out there?" Belafonte asked.

"I don't know—yet."

"Well, when are you gonna start trying to figure it out?" Belafonte said.

"I'll figure it out when the time comes."

"Do you know what they call a man who doesn't have a plan?" Bell said.

"Oh boy! Now here you go!" Damion said.

"They don't call him nothing. You understand? He's just in the way, taking up space and stealing good air."

A few days later, Belafonte told me about his conversation with Damion, but I was not surprised. In fact, I felt the tension between us gradually building up, and I had expected him to eventually get frustrated with me. I also began to sense that badgering him about what he should and shouldn't do wasn't good for either of us. If he wanted to be successful when he got out of prison, he would do everything possible to achieve that goal, and if he didn't, then that was on him.

We all need to sit alone sometimes and think about what we want to do with our lives and how we are going to get there. I describe it as time to quiet the mind. It's the time a person takes to reflect on his or her successes as well as their failures and focus on what, if any, changes need to be made.

Some of the best chess players I've ever met would get together in the prison library every Sunday morning to do battle on the chessboard. Being able to employ that competitive spirit felt good, and we all understood how enjoyable just this increment of freedom was. All of them were good, but there was one inmate from Queens, New York, whom all the chess players in Allenwood feared because of his high skill level. His name was Ace, and he was serving sixty years for distribution of crack cocaine. According to his grand jury indictment, he was buying kilos in New York from the Colombians and transporting them to North Carolina where he sold the drugs. Ace was a very serious character and a bit of an introvert sometimes. He knew chess moves that most of us weren't versed in, like his opening called the French Defense. Trying to figure it out would leave you scratching your head.

One Sunday morning, Ace and I were in the library sitting in front of the chessboard, playing an intense game, while nine other guys were standing around the table, watching us closely. About an hour into the match, my king got trapped in the corner by his two rooks, and I was two moves away from being checkmated.

"Your move," said Ace.

I didn't respond because I knew one of his tactics was to distract his opponent with meaningless conversation.

"If I were you, I would move the bishop first," Ace said again.

"I know what to do, man. I got this," I responded.

"Okay, okay. Just trying to help," Ace sarcastically said.

I was trapped and couldn't figure out a way to free my king, which is always bad news in a game of chess. After staring at the board for about ten minutes, I laid the king down on the chessboard, signaling to my opponent that I had resigned the game.

"Damn, son!" Ace said.

"You got me, bro," I said, admitting defeat. "I didn't have anywhere else to go."

Ace raised his arms in celebration of his victory. I had to give him credit; he was a skilled chess player. However, I wasn't a pushover myself.

"You're getting better, man," he said.

"I know," I responded confidently. Ace and I were rivals on the chessboard, but we also had a healthy amount of respect for each other.

"What's going on with you and your cellmate?" Ace inquired.

"What do you mean?" I asked.

"I haven't seen you two hanging out like before. He's been spending a lot of time with those Moorish Science brothers."

"He's doing his thing, man, and I have to do mine."

"I'm just saying, you two used to be tight," Ace remarked.

"He's got only a few months left, but he doesn't know how to stay off the radar, how to lay low and get the hell out of here, you know what I mean?"

"I feel you. I've got thirty-three years to go. Tell him I will switch places with him if he wants."

"He don't get it. Trust me," I replied.

"He reminds me of one of those stupid dudes out in the street. Motherfuckers who don't know how to quit while they're ahead," Ace remarked.

"What's happening with your appeal?" I inquired.

"I'm still waiting to hear back from the court. The prosecutor hasn't responded to the brief I filed," Ace explained.

"How's it looking?"

"I don't know. Once these people get their claws in you, it's hard to get them out. You'd think I committed murder the way they treat me."

"That's crazy."

"I see why you're frustrated with your homeboy. Don't forget to tell him what I said. I would trade places with him in a second."

My friends used to tell me that I was too serious at times, or too intense, and that I should relax more. However, they eventually learned that's just who I was as a person. So, when I was behind bars, this personal characteristic became even more pronounced due to the environment I was in. I refused to waste time; every minute of the day mattered. I really felt like I was in a life-or-death situation and couldn't afford to squander the free time I had.

In Allenwood, I became an avid reader of business books, with biographies and autobiographies being my favorites. I received many books from fellow inmates whose family members would mail them. After they finished reading them, they would pass them along to me. I loved reading about real people who had turned their lives around and achieved remarkable things. I was fascinated by their ability to discipline themselves, especially during challenging times. Their stories motivated me at a time when I desperately needed something to help me keep going.

In the prison library, a collection of biographies on Middle Eastern leaders and other prominent figures from around the world caught my attention. This collection of around twenty biographies was tucked away on a dusty shelf in the back of the library. I can't recall exactly what drew me to them, but something did. One of the books was about a political leader named Golda Meir, the first woman to become prime minister of Israel. As I dove into her story, I was captivated by her resilience under tremendous pressure. Born in Ukraine, she was raised and educated in America. The book detailed her many life challenges and the bias she faced on her journey to becoming the first female prime minister of Israel during a turbulent time in the Middle East. Rivals wanted to kill her simply because she was determined to make a difference in the world. One notable threat was a plan to assassinate the prime minister during her visit to the United States.

Other biographies in this collection of books included Menachem Begin, another influential political figure in Israel, as well as books on President Anwar Sadat of Egypt, the charismatic Palestinian leader Yasser Arafat, Bishop Desmond Tutu of South Africa, and the iconic world leader Nelson Mandela.

From my reading, I learned that decades ago, the signing of the Egypt-Israel Peace Treaty had been a tremendous international accomplishment. President Sadat and Menachem Begin were awarded the Nobel Peace Prize for their efforts to bring peace to the region back then. However, a few years later, during a parade in Egypt, Sadat was assassinated by officers in his own military while on live television. The betrayal by people so close to him shocked the world.

I had become enamored with self-education because I realized it was a process I could control. I didn't have to wait for someone else to teach me because I could teach myself. Many of the materials I discovered in the prison library would have never interested me while I was on the streets, but in prison, I was drawn to them like a magnet. Federal prison had become my version of Princeton University, University of Notre Dame, Stanford, and Brown University.

During another one of my library excursions, I found a book buried away on one of the dusty shelves that had a profound impact on me. The book was titled *Why Should White Guys Have All the Fun? How Reginald Lewis Created a Billion-Dollar Business Empire.* This book was inspirational on so many levels and became one of the most important pieces of literature I have ever read. Reginald F. Lewis was a savvy businessman from Baltimore and the first Black man in America to build a billion-dollar business. According to *Forbes* magazine, in 1992, Mr. Lewis was listed as one of the four hundred richest people in America. In 1983, he created a venture capital firm, and four years later, he bought Beatrice Foods, a beverage, snack food, and grocery store giant. This deal made him a legend in American business history. According to his book, he purchased sixty-four companies in thirty-one different countries, which was considered a conglomerate at the time. In the book, Mr. Lewis talked about the challenges he faced throughout his life, and I was astonished by his story. He was born and raised in Baltimore, Maryland, and attended Harvard Law School, where he earned his Juris Doctorate degree. He spoke a lot about how important family was to him and how that foundation provided stability in his life all the way back to when he was a child. One of his most famous quotes is, "Keep going, no matter what."

While I was reading that exhilarating piece of literature, the story of a man who made a difference in the world after making significant changes within himself, Damion burst into the cell.

*Boom!*

He slammed the heavy steel cell door shut, breaking my concentration. His timing couldn't have been worse. Immediately, I thought, *What's his problem now?*

He seemed agitated, but to be honest, I didn't want to get involved. I was trying to read, and by then, I had refocused my attention on the things I needed to do to help myself.

"This punk fouled me hard as hell on the court. He sleeps down in cell two-fourteen."

"What are you talking about, man?" I said.

"That dude from Pittsburgh! I'm waiting for Eric B to bring me a knife. I'm gonna handle him," Damion declared.

"Come on, man."

Suddenly, there was a knock on the door. It was Eric B, who had received an urgent message from another inmate that Damion needed to speak to him.

"Yo, they told me you needed the joint. What's going on?"

"It's that dude over in cell two-fourteen, Pittsburgh. I'm going to handle him."

"What happened?" Eric asked.

"He was fouling me hard as shit. Every time I went up for a shot, he slapped the hell out of me."

"Man, get out of here with that," Eric B said. "I was at the game, bro. You were playing him just as hard as he was playing you."

Eric B tried to reason with Damion, and I hoped he was listening. A pattern had developed where he was constantly on the verge of making one unwise decision after another. His anxiety seemed to be pushing him toward actions that could sabotage his chances of getting out of prison. That was my assumption, and it was the only explanation I had at the time.

"You need to chill. How much time you got left, anyway?" Eric B asked.

Damion didn't respond.

"I've been trying to tell him, but I think he wants to stay here with his Moorish Science brothers. He doesn't want to go home," I said.

"I ain't giving you no knife. I'm out of here," Eric B said.

Eric B left, and the evening ended that night with Damion avoiding the crime of attempted murder inside a federal prison. He didn't do anything that night that would have landed him in the isolation unit, which could have pushed back his release date by several months or years.

When you grow up in tough neighborhoods, you're taught not to tolerate disrespect, and I get it. But there are situations where you need to be smart. Eventually, I began to suspect that there was something more deeply wrong with Damion than just being agitated over a basketball game. Every other week, there was a different crisis requiring mediation, and I started to believe he was intentionally trying to ruin his chances of getting released.

It was strange because I observed him attempting to evolve, but I also saw his regressions over short periods. It was like he was trying to move forward, but something was pulling him back. There were even times when I thought he might be dealing with a chemical imbalance. He often talked about smoking weed and drinking alcohol with his friends when he was on the streets. Despite our unstable environment where guys frequently acted unpredictably, something just wasn't adding up.

However, I still had a few years left on my own prison sentence at the time, and every day needed to be about preparing for the future. One day, a friend of mine gave me valuable advice: "Before you save someone else, you have to save yourself." His advice was similar to the instructions flight attendants give passengers on a commercial flight before departure: "Please put your oxygen mask on first before helping others." February 2004 was a cold and windy month in the mountains of Central Pennsylvania. It was the same month I recovered from the swine flu that had swept through Allenwood, affecting inmates and guards alike. I had been sick for three weeks with a severe cough and a recurring fever that wouldn't go away. Then, as soon as I recovered, a prison guard came to my cell and told me to pack my belongings and prepare to be transferred to another prison.

I was in my cell packing my bags when I heard a loud knock on the door. It was Gee and Eric B.

"What's up, Kev?" Gee greeted me.

"Yo, what's the deal?" Eric B chimed in.

Gee and Eric B walked in, closing the door behind them.

"They're putting you on the bus? Where you headed?" Eric B asked.

"New Jersey," I replied.

"Damn, homie. Did you know they were transferring you?" Gee inquired.

"I put in for a transfer ten months ago," I explained while folding shirts and packing them into a green army duffle bag. "They have a good college program over there."

"Oh, okay. When Damion told us you were being transferred, I thought you'd pissed off Warden Keller again," Gee said.

I chuckled. "It wasn't like that. My counselor was just dragging his feet with my paperwork."

"You serious about that college stuff," Eric B said.

"I've got to have my mind right when I get out, man," I replied.

"I get it," Eric B acknowledged.

"Look out for Damion when I leave, alright?" I requested.

"I got him, man, but he better keep his butt off that damn basketball court. He ain't running up my sentence over some nonsense," Eric B asserted.

"Homie be acting crazy sometimes," Gee added.

"He don't understand how easy it is to get in trouble in this place. If you ain't careful, you can mess around and hurt somebody and never get out of here," Eric B warned.

"And I'm not with that," Gee affirmed.

"He's cool. He just needs some help," I said.

"Kev, you know how it is in here. You got to help yourself," Eric B emphasized.

The following day, I was loaded onto a prison bus, heading to my final destination in the federal prison system. The ride from Allenwood, Pennsylvania, to New Jersey, while shackled and chained, was mentally exhausting. I was on another road trip sponsored by the US government and the American taxpayer. The consolation prize was that I was one step closer to being a free man again. I knew that when I got out, I would face a tremendous challenge, but there was still plenty of time for me to prepare for that day. It was essential to take college courses and keep studying, but I also understood that I had to do more. I didn't want to be just another statistic, released from prison and stuck in some minimum-wage job or, worse, relying on the underground drug economy again for financial support. I didn't want Damion or me to be just another recidivism statistic on some government official's spreadsheet. Or some talking point for some politician campaigning on "Tough on Crime." Those were the harsh realities of being a formerly incarcerated person that I tried to convey to Damion. I didn't want either of us to become just another person who turned around and walked right back into the system after messing up.

As it's currently structured, the prison system isn't designed to help a person turn their life around. It's a warehousing system for individuals who haven't met society's standards. It's a place for those who society believes can't conform to the rules set forth by the governing bureaucracy.

The business of incarceration has become a profitable one too. Decades ago, the public was told that the purpose of incarceration was to punish individuals for their crimes and rehabilitate them into better human beings. But after the government began allowing for-profit companies to have access to cheap prison labor, the door to corruption swung wide open, and profits became the overarching priority, not rehabilitation. Just a few years ago, Victoria's Secret was using federal prison inmates to sew lingerie. And if you don't believe me, just Google it.

If an inmate doesn't commit to rehabilitating themselves while behind bars, it's unlikely they'll be able to navigate the challenges of surviving in America once they're released. Many of the necessary tools for making that transition aren't readily available, which is why the recidivism rate is so high.

But on July 20, 2004, Damion "Soul" Neal was released from Allenwood federal prison and returned to the streets of America. I can honestly say that he had the potential to be a contributor to society, not just a disruptor. However, it was also clear that he could be easily distracted and drawn into a negative space. If he could stay focused, he would be fine, but if not, he could run headfirst into a brick wall.

# CHAPTER 6

# GENERAL'S GREENE

THERE IS A BIG DIFFERENCE between winning a struggle and losing one. The first operative word, *winning*, can be breathtaking and exhilarating. It's often associated with success, achieving significant goals, and all those other phrases we use to describe victory. On the contrary, *losing* can be devastating to the human psyche, capable of stripping even the strongest man or woman of their dignity or even altering the course of their lives.

During my involvement in the underground drug economy, going to prison and then returning home was akin to receiving a badge of honor. In that environment it was viewed as equivalent to earning a medal in the military or obtaining a degree from a college or university. If you were fortunate enough to secure bail before serving your sentence, friends might even throw you a going-away party. Then, upon your release back into the community, you might be rewarded with a welcome-home party to celebrate your return. This dysfunction was disguised as winning, when in reality, we were losing badly, and the success we believed we had achieved was nothing more than a pipe dream.

On January 3, 2006, two years after Damion was released, I was released from a federal prison in New Jersey and returned home. The beauty of that moment lay in the opportunity for a fresh start. However, it didn't take long for me to realize that even when you retire from a life of crime, that dysfunctional mindset may still have a hold on you. You might still have a dysfunctional belief system and an irrational perspective on how the world operates beyond the street corner. From an outsider's perspective, it may appear that the recently released individual is "fixed" or he is "winning," but that might not be his reality. The allure of the drug trade can be just as addictive as the drugs themselves, especially when the only love you've ever known came from the streets. I was never a drug addict, but at times, I felt like one. I still had an insatiable craving for fast cars and fast money, and that monkey was still on my back. Physically, I was a free man, but mentally, I was still shackled and chained. I had to be vigilant to avoid stepping on the hidden minefields that seemed to be everywhere, or else I would find myself back in Allenwood. This is the part of a formerly incarcerated person's story that most people don't understand until the individual ends up back in an orange prison jumpsuit or their face appears on a wanted poster.

It wasn't until about two years after my release that I began to feel like my world was normalizing, and in my mind, I was making progress. I was in the process of rebuilding the life I had traded away for a cold, dark prison cell, and I was experiencing a sense of peace. All I wanted was to be an ordinary person in pursuit of the American Dream.

My mother and sister played a crucial role in supporting my reintegration into society, and I couldn't have achieved success without their support. Sometimes, it's not about having all the answers but it's about having the right people in your life with the right temperament while you search for those answers. Adapting to society after being away for so many years was a challenge, and some days proved harder than others. However, I can honestly say that having my family by my side made the transition significantly smoother.

I felt a profound sense of accomplishment in the positive turn my life had taken. It was the most uplifting feeling I had experienced in years, and I was determined to regain my "swagger." Reclaiming your "swagger" means trying to recapture the confidence you once possessed before it was abruptly taken from you. Returning to normalcy can be tough when you're still grappling with demons from your past. You may feel like you can "win," but that nagging voice of insecurity in your head persists, cautioning you with phrases like "don't trust it" or "watch your back."

Being incarcerated for an extended period had changed me in ways I hadn't fully comprehended. The fact that even after two years, I was still adjusting to seemingly trivial aspects of life was at times disconcerting. Two years later, I was still working on the little things and taking baby steps to get them right. Whether it meant holding a door open for a woman or simply greeting her with a smile, I needed practice. I was rusty, but I remained hopeful that, just like riding a bike, I would eventually regain my stride.

When I was away, I missed everything about losing my freedom, and that included being in the presence of a woman. I longed for the tantalizing scent of a woman and the texture of her hair. I missed seeing a woman in heels and a sleek dress; there's something undeniably alluring about that ensemble that a man who appreciates a woman's style cannot resist. I yearned for the sound of a woman's voice, even if, for some reason, it involved her 'telling me to "go to hell."' Yet, I also had to acknowledge that my track record in maintaining long-term relationships was far from flawless, and I needed to improve in that regard. In the past, I hadn't been as committed as I should have been, and I recognized the importance of working on this aspect of myself. The last thing I wanted was to make the mistake of entering a dysfunctional relationship that could derail the progress I had made up to that point. I felt like a changed man, but the true test had yet to come.

In addition to trying to regain my swagger, I had a much more important concern weighing on my mind. I needed to be acutely aware of how severe the HIV and AIDS epidemic had become in my community during my absence. I had undergone testing before my release from prison in New Jersey, which gave me 100 percent certainty that I didn't have the virus. However, I couldn't be as certain about the women I was meeting and dating. The dating scene felt like riding bumper cars at an amusement park, constantly getting jolted around by other cars until a direct hit left your vehicle disabled. Navigating this strange new world was still awkward at times. I struggled with how to have a mature conversation with a woman about her HIV status or lack thereof. It wasn't just a matter of asking if she had been tested; it also involved requesting to see the results for confirmation or even considering getting tested together. Two women I had dated years earlier had succumbed to the disease while I was in prison, and neither of them had appeared to be ill from what I had been told. Their deaths had been sudden, so I was proceeding with extreme caution.

By late 2008, I was carefully maneuvering through the complex landscape of what I described as a Free American Society. I was determined not to become entangled with people or situations that were not in my best interest. I reminded myself that people around the world make significant changes in their lives every day, so why couldn't I do the same? Change is always possible if you want it strongly enough. It's a natural part of life, flowing like water in every corner of the earth.

In January 2009, I found myself playing the role of a baker in the kitchen of my apartment on the northwest side of town. I had stumbled upon a new hobby—making cheesecake pies with graham cracker crusts, covered in bright red cherry filling, and topped with Cool Whip. Why cheesecake? I have no idea how it began; it was just one of those quirky hobbies that evolved over time. I became somewhat of an amateur dessert chef, specializing in a dish that would be a nightmare for diabetics, despite its deliciousness. My health was excellent, and if I were to meet an early demise, indulging in cheesecake until my arteries froze didn't seem like a bad way to go.

I would prepare these delectable desserts on Sunday mornings just before watching NFL football games, which dominated the day for millions of Americans. This was long before Colin Kaepernick began to kneel during the National Anthem. Many things had changed in my life, but my love for watching professional sports on television remained constant. It wasn't the worst way for a former-inmate-turned-upstanding-citizen to spend his Sunday afternoons. It was just another labor of love for a man who was doing his best to stay on the straight and narrow.

In the past, I had cooked in the kitchen, but it had been for a different purpose—preparing kilos of heroin from the Bronx for the streets. But those days were long behind me, and I had transformed into a gentle giant. The word on the streets was that the former heroin dealer from the west side had retired from the game. Most people who knew me well understood that my new life was not a contrived story to appease my parole officer; it was genuine. I had put an end to selling opiates to people struggling with addiction. Nevertheless, some of my former associates remained skeptical and didn't believe in the new and improved Kevin Shird. I began to hear rumors like, "He's gone soft." There were even comments suggesting, "He's talking all this change shit now, like Obama."

To be completely honest, there were moments when the offensive talk nearly pushed me to my breaking point. There were nights when I contemplated donning all-black attire and heading down to the old neighborhood to see what the guy with the big mouth really had to say. There were times when I thought about driving over to the west side to have a face-to-face conversation with Judas. I even entertained thoughts of settling old scores with individuals who failed to repay debts from years past, when I supplied them with goods before my sudden departure. At one point, I even considered launching a "Pay Or Else" hashtag campaign on Facebook just to grab the attention of the nonbelievers. However, I wasn't a sociopath, and I really was a changed man. In the words of Nelson Mandela, "Here is a man who has learned to control his anger, discipline his pain, and channel his desire for revenge." So, I maintained my composure, recognizing that this was merely a test and not worth jeopardizing the substantial progress I had achieved thus far.

With one hand on the Bible and the other on the Quran, I took a deep breath and suppressed my grievances. According to the street code, when someone slanders you, it's expected to retaliate without restraint, but I had grown beyond the code of the streets; I wanted to live by a different set of principles. I came to understand that the street code was just an illusion, diluted like a poorly mixed drink at a cheap bar. It didn't offer love or redemption, and I had to come to terms with that.

As time passed, I remained committed to the philosophy of change, convinced that I had things all figured out. I often told myself, "I think I've got it now." If I continued to trust the process, the other pieces of my life would fall into place. I felt confident about the future, and it seemed like I had found the answer to the puzzle. Ironically, these were the same affirmations I used to navigate life behind bars, where trouble loomed around every corner. If I could survive in that unstable environment, where chaos was the norm, life on the outside should be a breeze.

I also realized that if I wanted to achieve anything significant, I needed to fully commit to it. I needed to stay focused on moving forward, not looking back. Someone once said, "You can have a million great ideas, but they're worthless if you don't act on at least one of them." To achieve my goals, I had to concentrate on the task at hand; this was basic knowledge that I understood and needed to apply. The practice phase was over, and the real game had begun. Life would throw fastballs at me at 90 mph, and I had a choice: hit a home run and win or strike out and lose—again.

By spring that year, I embarked on the challenging journey of writing a manuscript. It wasn't much of a stretch, as I had discovered my aptitude for writing while taking college courses in Allenwood. As I worked on the manuscript, I also realized that writing was therapeutic in ways I hadn't understood before. People had often said to me, "You should write a book someday. You've had a crazy life." These comments were frequent, even from strangers I would meet. So I heeded their advice and set out on the path to becoming an author. At the time, I didn't know if I wanted to be like Ernest Hemingway, Langston Hughes, or Ta-Nehisi Coates, but I knew I wanted to create a consequential piece of literature.

Initially, maintaining a consistent writing routine posed a challenge. I would start forming ideas and thoughts, only to become frustrated and walk away from my laptop or notepad. Developing the story and characters proved daunting. However, I eventually realized that all I needed to do was document my life as it had happened. My story, no matter how painful, was authentic, and I didn't need to embellish it. I was simply a recorder of history, and as I started writing, to my surprise, it became easier. Words and sentences flowed onto the pages like waves crashing onto the shore.

In a world filled with distractions, it's easy to lose focus on our goals. However, staying committed to the bigger picture, even if it means sitting alone in a quiet room, is essential for progress. Actor Denzel Washington once said, "Dreams without goals are just dreams and ultimately they fuel disappointments. On the road to achieving your dreams, you must apply discipline, but more importantly, consistency."

Once I overcame the challenge of staying focused on my goals, I encountered another hurdle: opening up and being transparent. Although I had left the streets behind long ago, I still sometimes reverted to my old street mentality, particularly when it came to sharing my vulnerabilities. However, as a writer, I had to change that mindset and embrace transparency by sharing stories about my pain and experiences.

I was deeply committed to the success of this project. It marked a new journey for me, and I felt an obligation to be completely honest with the readers who I knew would scrutinize every word and phrase. I anticipated questions like, "What did you mean by that?" or, "Did that really happen?" If I was going to take this trip down memory lane, I had to do it with complete honesty and unburdened transparency. It was a significant leap, but a necessary one if I wanted to create a piece of literature that people could genuinely appreciate. Seasoned readers can easily spot insincerity in an author's work, and I was determined that this book would not appear that way.

I had no intention of glamorizing the street life that had wrecked so many lives, nor did I want to give the impression that I had always reveled in that world, because I didn't. While there were moments when I enjoyed the perks that came with being in the drug trade, it's not a career I would ever recommend to anyone. Some days, as I wrote, I found myself an emotional wreck, penning down past misdeeds that the world would one day critique. From the librarian to the mailman, my life would be a literal open book for anyone interested in reading about it.

One day, while writing at home, something struck me. I recalled my younger self as a rap music aficionado, listening to rap lyrics religiously. It was during the freestyle era, with rap icons like Tupac and Biggie Smalls dominating the airwaves. Back then, I was captivated by their lyrics, and there were times when I would listen to those booming beats for hours on end. So, I devised a method to transport myself back to that era and to help me write authentically about those years. I hoped it would rekindle my memories and spark my creativity. I found a vintage record store selling 1990s CDs, featuring the hardcore music I used to listen to when I felt invincible. Reacquainting myself with those hit records brought back vivid memories of my days as a street leader and significantly aided my writing.

I also employed other techniques to jog my memories of the not-so-good old days. I'd hop in my car and drive through the dilapidated neighborhoods where I once spent a great deal of time. I would park there on the corner next to the decrepit shells of dwellings that resembled war-torn Iraq and reminisce about a tumultuous time. While sitting there, I could feel the ghosts of the drug runners who used to yell "Five-O" when plainclothes narcotics detectives drove down Fayette Street in unmarked police cars. I was reminded of the summer days when scores of heroin addicts would stand out in the hot sun waiting for the new package to arrive. It was a feeling of déjà vu. I envisioned stickup boys lying in the shadows of the open-air drug market with nine-millimeter handguns held tightly in their hands, waiting to commit a heist. I saw images of the bullet-riddled corpses that were taken away in ambulances as loud sirens blared through Mount Street. And as I dove deeper just to write about those ugly days of old, it occurred to me that those encounters that were often violent were still heavy on my heart.

One day, while at home in my living room, I was writing another chapter for the manuscript, recounting a shootout I had been involved in with a member of a rival drug crew. As I continued to write about this incident, I recognized just how incredibly dangerous, foolish, and stupid it had been. Several years had passed since then, and I hadn't thought much about it until I began writing. That's when the scab on that old wound was ripped off. Our minds have a way of burying traumatic memories, almost as if they never happened. But while sitting there with my pen and notepad, tears started flowing from my eyes. I was alone, trying to maintain my composure, and I wasn't entirely sure why I was so affected by this old memory. It really shook me. Then I realized that I was distressed because I could have accidentally harmed an innocent child walking down the street that day, or I could have lost my own life. I definitely wasn't upset that I didn't let some sociopath just blow my brains out—somehow it was something much deeper.

A few days later, I confided in a friend who works in the mental health services field about that experience. I also told her that I was still having trouble sleeping at night and that sometimes I would have crazy nightmares. She suggested that these things could be symptoms of post-traumatic stress disorder (PTSD) and she recommended seeking professional counseling.

"You were exposed to a traumatic event during the shooting, and even after all these years, there may well be lingering effects."

"You mean I'm going crazy?"

"No, boy!" she said.

She reassured me that I was not going insane and suggested that I speak to someone who had experience working in mental health and trauma.

I was surprised, but the more I thought about it, the more it made sense. I had heard the term *PTSD* used at a conference. I also learned a little about it while watching news reports about military soldiers who had fought in Afghanistan and Iraq and had been diagnosed with the disorder. But this was the first time I had ever heard it applied to events that occurred here in the streets of America. At the time it was still a subject that no one I knew talked much about, but slowly I was putting the pieces together.

A few weeks later, I stubbornly and reluctantly took my friend's advice. I was working for a nonprofit organization that provided its employees with good health insurance. So, I was able to make an appointment to see a psychologist where my insurance would cover the costs.

The psychologist I met with was a tall white man in his early sixties who seemed like a pleasant guy. Several plaques and degrees hung on the wall in his office, including some from Yale and Princeton, so he seemed experienced in the profession. At the start of our meeting, he was very cordial.

"It's great to meet you, Kevin. So, tell me a little about yourself," he said.

"Well, I grew up here. In school, I was a pretty good student, but things got off track when I got to high school. I started selling drugs when I was about sixteen. In the streets, I saw a lot of crazy stuff. In fact, there's very little I haven't seen. I could write a long list of friends who've been either shot or killed. Back then it seemed normal, you know what I mean?" I said.

It felt odd talking to a perfect stranger this way, but I was committed to doing whatever I needed to do to help myself. I realized I had problems, and I also realized that I could not solve them on my own.

"I spent almost twelve years in prison in some really tough places. Most of the time was in the federal system, but I also spent a few years in California state, which was nuts. I'm not sure what was worst, the confinement or seeing so many crazy things happening around me. The prison environment is its own little crazy world, man. You know what I mean?" I said.

I was trying to be transparent so that he would understand who I was and what I had been through.

"My father was a chronic alcoholic and my parents divorced when I was young. Back then I didn't understand what alcohol addiction meant and how it affected families. I think that might have been one of the things that drove me out in the streets at such an early age."

After I spoke for several minutes, I sat there, the room feeling awkwardly silent. The psychologist stared at me and did not say a word. I was thinking, *Well, aren't you going to say something?* Then, he said, "Interesting" and not much else. This interaction, or lack thereof, went on for almost an hour, then he looked at his watch, stood up and said, "Thanks, Mister Shird. See you next week." And that's when I left.

The only word I can think of to describe him now is *oafish*. I definitely would not describe him as a seasoned mental health professional like the degrees hanging on his office wall suggested. There was a disconnect that could not be swept under the rug. It felt like *white centering*, a term used to describe the belief that white culture, values, and norms are the center of the world. I don't know if his response or lack thereof was intentional, but after opening up to this complete stranger, it was not the response I expected. I don't know if he was tone deaf or just lacked empathy. I just felt like we did not connect with each other and that he could not feel my pain. Everything about our interaction seemed awkward.

Initially, I believed that my first experience with a psych would be like in the movies where the patient lies down on a sofa, spills his guts, and a short time later, I'd find myself cured; no more abusing sex, drugs, or rock 'n' roll. But that did not happen. Instead, I left his office that day just as confused as I was before I got there. Generally, most men will not talk about their mental health status, and especially a guy from the streets. It's almost unheard of unless he is backed into a corner and literally forced to do so. It's as rare as a unicorn walking through Central Park in New York. And I did not take him up on his offer to return the following week, because I didn't feel like it was a genuine offer. I did not feel like he was the person that could help me understand and manage what I was going through. I didn't know what to do at that point, so I went back to square one, which was: whatever I was going through I can handle it because I'm a man and men can handle anything, right?

A short time later, I went back to writing, and it seemed as if that was the only therapy I needed. I wasn't sure why, but writing was the one thing that made me feel at peace. The details of those old encounters in the streets were no longer buried away, but they had come alive on the pages of a piece of literature. The stories I was writing were gritty and grimy, but they were the truth about the road I had traveled. I was writing about how the sausage was made in the factory of the underground drug economy, and I was exposing the ugliness that lies there. And for some strange reason, it felt good in a way that nothing else did. It felt better than taking drugs. It felt better than drinking alcohol. And it certainly felt better than sitting in front of some old insensitive white man who I barely knew while spilling my guts.

After a few months, my writing skills began to evolve, and my manuscript began to turn into an inexact flower full of odd colors and beautifully deformed leaves. It was like looking at the sonogram photo of an unborn child. Before the child is born, you fall madly in love with this imperfect picture that you hope will, one day, turn out to be a bit more attractive.

One Sunday afternoon, I was buried deep inside my one-bedroom apartment. I was on my laptop writing and listening to Rihanna on Pandora Music. It was just another day in the office, another habit I had grown accustomed to, and I was enjoying every second of it. The words were shining bright like diamonds, and all I could think about was creating a bestseller and thus creating a legacy that matters.

I was dating a woman around this same time who I really liked, but she dumped me. She told me that I was spending too much time writing. "All you do is sit around on this stupid computer writing. I can't deal with this. We're done!" She said.

I probably could have put more effort into holding onto the relationship, but I did not. I had to make a choice, and I chose building a future for myself. I had become a recluse who was addicted to composing words and paragraphs from morning until night, and it felt better than everything else.

The manuscript was becoming filled with intricate details that I still wasn't sure I wanted to share with the world. But then, I was reminded of all the men I had met during my years in prison. Some of them were serving fifty, sixty, and even seventy-year prison sentences for nonviolent drug offenses. Some of them would never see the streets again; some would not get out until they were old men, and some would die there. Many of them had appealed their convictions and had been waiting years for a response on whether their sentences would be reduced. Some were the casualties of the War on Drugs, which dated back to a time when the Bush administration had no idea what they were doing when they implemented draconian laws in the name of America's Crack Cocaine Lie. For almost fifty years, the federal government has been carrying out a campaign that has made criminals out of millions of people. The War on Drugs, while entirely ineffective at reducing the distribution or consumption of dangerous illegal substances, has been incredibly effective at funneling minority groups into prisons. I had a rare opportunity to write about some of the injustices they faced, so I thought maybe I should take advantage of this moment.

That day, I thought a lot about the guys I used to sit with at the cafeteria table in Allenwood, guys like Belafonte, Eric B, and Gee. I even thought about the guys I played chess with in the prison library, like Ace. I began to wonder how they were faring in the snowy mountains of Central Pennsylvania. Then, I thought about my former cellmate, Damion "Soul" Neal, and wondered how he was doing since being released. It had been a few years since I'd last seen him, so I assumed that he'd had plenty of time to re-establish himself in the community. By now, he should have found a job and settled in. In Allenwood, he talked a lot about his daughter, so I hoped he was happy to be back in her life. I also recalled him telling me that he wanted to move to Atlanta, Georgia, to rebuild his life and focus on music production. I did not have his telephone number, nor did I have any other way to get in touch with him. When I left Allenwood, we were not on the best of terms, so we did not exchange contact information. I had no idea where to begin looking for him, but I figured I could find something by doing a Google search. In this world of information at your fingertips, I thought it would be the best way to find a lead.

I typed Damion's name into the search engine on my laptop and then sat there waiting for the results. I was looking forward to catching up with him and talking about all the bizarre things that went on in Allenwood. I figured we would laugh and joke about those days but also talk about our new lives since leaving that harsh place. Had he been successful in pursuing his dream of producing music? Had he bought a house, opened a bank account, or travelled the world?

The Google search was processing slowly and had not revealed any information, so I checked to make sure I had his name spelled correctly. It also was not helpful that my neighbor's Wi-Fi signal, which I was tapping into, had a slow connection, so I waited patiently. Then, a search result appeared on my computer screen, but as I read it, I was confused. Information about someone with the name Damion Neal appeared, but the headline did not make sense. The search result read: "Accused Murderer's Car Found in County." I was baffled, then I began reading the next search result: "Damion Neal Is Being Sought in Connection with Homicide Investigation."

I was stunned, and I was trying to understand what I had stumbled across. Then, I spotted another headline from the *Dover Post* newspaper titled "Man Arrested in General's Greene Double Murder." As I read the article, I learned that Damion had been arrested in Delaware and charged with double homicide. According to the article, he had been accused of killing his former girlfriend and her new boyfriend inside the bedroom of her home.

An article in the *Dover Post* written by staff writer Melissa Steele and posted online on November 11, 2008, read:

### Man Arrested in General's Greene Double Murder

A woman and her boyfriend were allegedly shot dead by the woman's ex-boyfriend Nov. 9 in the master bedroom of her General's Greene residence. Delaware State Police almost immediately identified the suspect as Damion Neal, 32, and began a search for him, said police spokesperson Cpl. Jeffrey Whitmarsh. A few hours earlier, Whitmarsh said troopers had responded to the home in connection with a domestic dispute wherein Neal had confronted the ex-girlfriend, Tonessa Barlow, about not answering his phone calls. Neal allegedly damaged Barlow's front door and fled when she called 911. Police then searched for him at his known hangouts and even spoke to him on the cell phone at one point, but Whitmarsh said they were unable to find him. Whitmarsh said Neal borrowed a friend's car and returned a few hours later. He allegedly entered the house and went to the master bedroom where he shot and killed Barlow and her new boyfriend, Richard Tolson, 29, of Dover. Neal then fled to the Baltimore area where authorities from the Maryland police and the U.S. Marshals Task Force arrested him.[2]

The internet is a place where you can find information on almost anything. Sometimes you may have to work a little harder to find it, but eventually you will. In this instance, there were several articles online about this incident. ABC Channel 47 WMDT filed the following report:

Delaware State Police say they arrested the man who shot and killed two Dover residents over the weekend. Joan Collins cannot believe what happened in her neighborhood on Saturday. Police say they first came to this house for a domestic dispute between Tonessa Barlow and her ex-boyfriend Damion Neal. But they say Neal got away before they got there. Corporal Bruce Harris says, "He had actually done damage to the door, and he was harassing her as well." Police issued arrest warrants for Neal, but they say they saw no signs of him until later that night. Sometime after midnight, Police say Neal came back to the house,

---

2   Melissa Steele, "Man Arrested in General's Greene Double Murder," *Dover Post*, November 10, 2008, https://www.delawareonline.com/story/news/2008/11/11/man-arrested-in-general-s/63990739007/.

snuck inside and up to the bedroom. They say he then shot and killed Barlow and her new boyfriend. Collins says she is shocked by the news, but she says she did hear a lot of commotion. She says, "I didn't hear any gunshots, but I just heard maybe he fell down the stairs and was trying to get against the wall, because he kept banging." The next day, Collins discovered what had happened. She says, "I want to get out of here, but my husband doesn't want to move."

After reading several articles, I found myself sitting on the edge of my chair, gazing at the recently purchased Hewlett Packard laptop, feeling numb. As I continued to digest the details of the crime, an unsettling feeling grew in the pit of my stomach. This act of violence was something I struggled to comprehend. The first question that crossed my mind: "Why would Damion do this?" The second: "Why do I care so much about his problems?"

There was also a part of me that wished I had never conducted that Google search. Various scenarios regarding what might have happened raced through my mind. Was Damion capable of committing such a cold-blooded murder, or had the charges against him been fabricated? None of it seemed to make sense. However, the more I delved into the news reports, the more I realized the gravity of the situation.

For a moment, I hoped that the accused man wasn't the same Damion Neal I had known. What if the police had arrested the wrong person? Had a corrupt officer framed him, as we've seen in many other criminal cases across the country? Was it a setup, with a corrupt law enforcement official planting evidence to implicate Damion? If so, his lawyers could rectify the situation, and he would be cleared before the trial even began.

Then, another troubling thought crossed my mind. Could Damion have been so deeply affected by his breakup with his former girlfriend that he snapped? I couldn't fathom why he would do something so irrational, but the more I read the articles, the more I understood the dire predicament faced by my former cellmate.

According to news reports, the homicides took place inside a townhouse in General's Greene, a low-income housing community that had once been the residence of Damion's ex-girlfriend. General's Greene was located just off Route 1 in Dover, near the Dover Air Force Base. Because I had a personal connection with Damion, my interest in the case was high.

As my interest grew, the amateur journalist within me sprang into action. I had been working on a book and conducting extensive research for months, so delving into Damion's case didn't feel like a significant departure. I continued my online investigations, uncovering more and more details. That's when I stumbled upon some astonishing comments in the Topix.com comment section, a Delaware online blog.

On the blog, a person with the username "Tish" wrote: *"He was a nice and outspoken person. This is not something he would do. He was just a positive person who always had great advice about life. I miss you."*

This comment by "Tish" about her interactions with Damion was a reminder to me of the guy I once knew. This was the guy I remembered having long conversations with about his positive outlook on life. This was the guy I remembered talking to in Allenwood about what he wanted to do when he got out of prison. I saw the guy who, at one point, wanted to do the right thing, but what happened?

There was another comment written on the same blog by someone with the username "Nick" who seemed adamant that Damion was not the killer, *"He ain't do no crazy stuff like that. He got mad respect for girls, that ain't him."*

As I continued to read the comments, I noticed that there were several people posting on the blog who said they knew Damion personally. Someone with the username "Sandra" wrote, *"He was in my English class last semester at Delaware Tech."* One of the comments were especially painful to read. The person who posted this remark went by the username "Desia" and she identified herself as Damion's daughter: *"This is my father I wouldn't believe it, but his girlfriend was murdered, and I did know her but please do not leave any negative things about him."* If in fact this was Damion's daughter commenting on the blog, she had to be devastated by the allegations leveled against her father.

There was another comment posted on the blog by someone with the username "Ann": *"To Desia, I feel for you and your family. I know you are too young to understand, and I understand he is your father. But Tonessa and Richard had children. They lost their mother. So, let's have a heart for their children who lost their mother. I knew Tonessa and my heart goes to their families. So please let's not sugar coat what Damion has done. I mean who are the victims here? Maybe he will get the help he needs, while serving a life sentence. I knew Damion and he has a bad temper."*

And after reading the following post written by a person with the username "Tomeya," my heart was heavy for her. *"The woman he killed was my mommy."* If that really was the daughter of the deceased woman, it had to be unsettling for her to see what was being written on the blog.

After reading these posts, I began to understand the emotional impact the crimes had on the people inside the Dover, Delaware, community. There were some leaving commentary who thought highly of Damion, like the person who said they attended college classes with him. But then there were others who had an opposing view of him, like the person with the username "Ann" who posted, *"I knew Damion and he has a bad temper."*

Ironically, Ann's comment matched the description of the man I knew very well. I had witnessed his temper erupt in Allenwood over seemingly trivial issues, while in his mind, they were of utmost importance.

I had no idea why Damion had gone to Delaware, as I was certain he had returned to Maryland after leaving Allenwood. I couldn't recall him ever mentioning Dover during our time together. Did he have family living there that he never talked about? It was possible, but I had no concrete information. I didn't know how he had ended up there, but while conducting further online research, I stumbled upon court documents that shed some light on the matter.

According to a federal court filing dated January 24, 2006, titled "Probation Jurisdiction Transferred to District of Delaware as to Damion Neal," the document revealed that Damion had gone through the proper legal channels to transfer his federal probation for the handgun case he had served time for in Allenwood. According to the document, US District Court Judge Garbis found that Damion had complied with all his probation requirements and subsequently allowed him to transfer his probation to Dover, Delaware.

So, at some point, Damion was indeed meeting the requirements set by the courts and his probation officer, or at least it appeared that way. It was also documented in the court record that Damion was attending college classes at Delaware Technical Community College in Dover. I was glad to see he had at least pursued his education.

Neither the judge nor his probation officer would have permitted him to leave Maryland if they didn't believe he was complying with the terms of his probation. So, at some point, Damion seemed to have been in the right state of mind. However, the question remained: how had things gone so terribly wrong?

Periodically, I would check online to see how his criminal case was progressing through the courts. I searched the internet for updates, but for several months, there were no changes noted. Murder trials often take a considerable amount of time to move through the court system, and Damion's case was no exception. While his situation did not consume my life, I did have concerns about his well-being. In a strange way, I felt somewhat responsible for his return to prison. What if I had continued to stay in contact with him after my transfer from Allenwood? Could I have had a more positive impact on his life? What if I had stayed in touch when he was released? Would it have made a difference?

I hoped that, just maybe, he was innocent of the charges and could get another chance at a normal life. In the back of my mind, I remembered that I had seen individuals acquitted of murder before, so there was a chance, I supposed. Was it possible he was not guilty? I didn't want to see anyone I knew in this kind of trouble, but if he had committed those crimes, there would be a tremendous price to pay.

One evening, I was at home in my apartment, sitting on the sofa, and watching television. I was channel surfing, trying to find a reason to justify paying for an overpriced cable package with two hundred channels I never watched. I switched from the Discovery Channel to HBO and then to some obscure sports channel featuring a ping-pong tournament in Tokyo. As I continued to navigate, I landed on CNN, which had a "Breaking News" banner running across the bottom of the screen. And wouldn't you know it, John Allen Muhammad, the convicted DC Sniper who had terrorized the nation in 2002 with his violence, had just been executed by officials in the state of Virginia.

One of his attorneys, J. Wyndal Gordon, Esq., told reporters that Muhammad's last meal had been chicken with red sauce and cake. According to Gordon, he had spent several hours with Muhammad in the days leading up to his execution. He was also in the room when Muhammad received the lethal injection of potassium chloride and other drugs that ended his life. I had no idea why this case and this man kept appearing on my radar over the years, but it did. Maybe it was some kind of omen. A few years after Muhammad's execution, I met his former attorney, J. Wyndal Gordon, and we became good friends. You could look at Muhammad's case from various perspectives. Some people have labeled him a monster, while others describe him as insane. Even one of his own lawyers said that he was a "delusional" man. But what I wanted to know was how this man had evolved the way he had. I was wondering the same thing about Damion.

# CHAPTER 7

# THE ROOM WHERE IT HAPPENS

THE DISTANCE BETWEEN BALTIMORE AND Dover spans approximately 107 miles. According to law enforcement officials, Damion exported violence from his hometown to Delaware, where he committed murder. Taking another human being's life is always a grave matter, but in this case, it was nothing short of unimaginable. It involved the execution of an innocent woman and her boyfriend at the hands of a former lover. Such actions are something that the majority of people would never contemplate, but it's that small segment of our society that carries out a significant portion of the violence in America.

We're often shocked and appalled by the violence we see in our country, but hypocritically we are obsessed with watching violent acts on television and on movie screens while savoring every minute of it. We condemn it but only for a moment before we look at it again, and again, and again. Damion's case was not a movie or one of many popular television shows like *Breaking Bad* or *The Blacklist* that viewers enjoy watching. Scenes from those shows are choreographed by actors who rise from the dead after a violent scene is filmed. This case in Dover was a real crime, not entertainment. It was an act where anger and rage journeyed off to the dark side to kill. It was the case of a man who gazed at the faces of two innocent victims while wielding a handgun in his cold bare hands.

The woman shot and killed by Damion was Tonessa Barlow, his former girlfriend. At the time of the murder, she resided at 2050 General's Way, the very scene of the crime. Tonessa was a vibrant thirty-four-year-old woman, known for her love of dancing, reading, and good music. An acquaintance mentioned her passion for the New England Patriots, suggesting she would have celebrated the numerous Super Bowl rings won by Tom Brady over the years. Tonessa was a fun-loving young woman who cherished summer barbeques with her family and friends. At the time of her death, she left behind four children and even had two grandchildren. Although she might have seemed young to be a grandmother, she was a deeply family-oriented person. Her passing devastated her twelve brothers and eleven sisters, as well as numerous cousins, nephews, aunts, and uncles in her large and close-knit family.

Richard Tolson was Tonessa's boyfriend, and he too tragically lost his life during the General's Greene homicides. Richard was affectionately known as "Lil Rick" by his family and friends. He was only twenty-nine years old when he met his untimely demise. He was a young man who had his entire life ahead of him, a future that was abruptly taken away. He left behind a young son who would never have the opportunity to spend quality time with his father. The child would never experience the joy of playing catch with his dad or simply taking a leisurely stroll in the park. Sadly, they would miss out on the daily pleasures in life that many of us take for granted.

Much like Tonessa, Richard came from a large and loving family. He had six brothers and four sisters who held him close to their hearts. Additionally, he left behind one aunt, seven uncles, and a total of thirty nieces and nephews scattered throughout his hometown. Friends deeply cherished

Richard both within and outside of Dover. During his youth, he attended the local middle school and high school, and he later pursued his education at Delaware Technical Community College, where coincidentally Damion was also a student.

According to Delaware State Police Detective Paskevicius, the horrifying events took place on November 9, 2008. Damion entered Tonessa's residence at approximately 3:00 a.m. and committed the murders. Detective Paskevicius was called in by Lieutenant Fraley to assist with the homicide investigation and arrived at the crime scene at 2050 General's Way around ten thirty that morning. After a briefing from Fraley, he meticulously examined the crime scene while taking notes.

Shortly thereafter, Detective Paskevicius was informed that a witness named Linda was waiting at the station to report the theft of her vehicle. Linda happened to be Damion's girlfriend at the time of the murders. During her interview at the station, Linda disclosed that "he dated Tonessa prior to dating me, but they broke up two years ago." She also informed the detective that Damion was still involved in an ongoing relationship with Tonessa.

"I dropped him off at Delaware Technical Community College on Saturday at around nine o'clock," Linda recounted. "When I returned to pick him up, a friend of his had to assist him in getting into the car because he was injured." According to Linda, earlier that day, Damion had been involved in a physical altercation with Richard, which had left Damion's face visibly bruised and battered. The altercation revolved around the dysfunction in his relationship with Tonessa.

"I dropped him off at my house and then went to play bingo with some friends. After returning home later, I parked my car in the driveway. That was the last time I saw it. Damion and I went to sleep, but when I woke up, he was gone, my car was missing from the driveway, and the keys were nowhere to be found," she added.

Her handgun was also missing, and beside herself, Damion was the only person aware of where the firearm was stored in the home. She also informed the detective that she had called Damion's cell phone that morning and had spoken to him several times, but he refused to disclose his whereabouts.

So, what prompted law enforcement officials to go to the home where the tragic killings had taken place? According to the police, a friend of Tonessa's arrived at the house that morning to pick up her child, who had spent the night there. Upon her arrival, she noticed that the front door was slightly ajar, which raised some concern. She decided to enter the home, proceeded upstairs, and discovered the bodies of Tonessa and Richard in the bedroom. Frightened, she swiftly collected her child and hurried to her own residence down the street, where she dialed 911 to inform the authorities of the horrifying discovery.

"I just went to my cousin's and the door was open and I went in there and she is not breathing," the witness said to the 911 operator.

"Did you see any blood...?" The 911 operator asked.

"No, I didn't see no blood or nothing, but she's freezing cold."

"Can you go back up there where she is at?"

"Yeah, I'll go back but I'm scared."

"We're going to send help right over there, okay. But we need to get her some help, okay? Is it possible for you to go [back] up there with that phone or not?"

"I'm on my mom's phone instead of mine. The reason I went over there [was] because she had the baby. She's lying on the floor and her boyfriend is lying on the bed. I called both their names and then I stood up and they're cold—their hands are cold. They're not breathing or nothing." She said.

"Neither one of them?" the operator asked.

"I was smacking them and hitting them and they're not waking up. And their hands are stiff and cold."

"Do you want to try CPR?"

"I don't know how," the witness replied.

Despite her emotional state, the witness returned to the crime scene and waited outside while on the phone with the emergency operator. A few minutes later, Delaware State Police and paramedics arrived. After the home was thoroughly searched by law enforcement officials for any sign of a suspect, paramedics were granted access. They confirmed that the two victims discovered in the bedroom had succumbed to their injuries. Five of the six shots fired into the bedroom had struck Tonessa and Richard, resulting in their deaths. Police later located spent .380 caliber shell casings near the victims.

Dover is a very small city, so, it did not take long for news to spread that there had been a double homicide. Tonessa's sister learned of the murders and rushed to her sister's home, which by then had become a crime scene. She informed the officers on-site that Tonessa and Damion had been in an "on again, off again" relationship for three years and that she was aware of an altercation between Richard and Damion the previous day. She also mentioned seeing a bite mark on Richard's cheek, which he confirmed had resulted from his altercation with Damion. Subsequently, she provided the officers with contact numbers for Damion and a member of his family living in Maryland.

Around 11:00 a.m., an officer standing at the scene was approached by a neighbor residing down the street. The neighbor informed the officer that she had discovered a Delaware State identification card lying in the parking lot near her home. She explained that she noticed law enforcement officials responding to the emergency call, so she picked up the ID and instinctively brought it to the officer. The identification card belonged to Damion Neal.

At approximately 11:30 a.m., a detective from the Delaware State Police conducted an interview with a friend of Tonessa's inside his patrol car. She recounted that Tonessa had informed her that Damion had been at her house on November 8 and had "instigated trouble" with her new boyfriend. She went on to explain that when Damion and Richard became involved in a physical altercation, Tonessa had called the police. However, by the time the officers arrived, Damion had vanished.

Later that evening, Tonessa and some friends went to a bar where they met up with Richard. Then, the three of them got into her vehicle and drove around looking for things to do before deciding to go to her god sister's house. They spent time there drinking and listening to music and departed around midnight. Afterwards, they returned to General's Greene, where Tonessa's friend dropped Tonessa and Richard off and their friend proceeded home.

The bodies were discovered at nine o'clock that morning, and developments in the case began swiftly unfolding. Not only did the police have the name of a suspect, but they also possessed his identification card and telephone numbers. Around 2:00 p.m., a detective was in communication with a family member of Damion's residing in Baltimore. The detective had previously called one of the numbers provided by Tonessa's sister and left a message. Shortly thereafter, a woman returned his call and informed him that Damion was with her and would willingly surrender to the authorities. A few hours later, Damion turned himself in to the United States Marshal Service in Baltimore and was taken into custody.

After spending a few days in Baltimore, law enforcement officials transported Damion back to Delaware, where Detective Michael Maher interrogated him inside an interview room at the same police station where Linda, his girlfriend, had been interviewed. The interrogation room was small, with plain white walls and a single table and two chairs positioned in the center, the lighting was bright, casting harsh shadows and adding to the tense atmosphere.

"I'm Detective Maher, and I'm with the Delaware State Police Homicide Unit. I've been assigned to this case, and I've been working on it since Sunday," Detective Maher said to Damion.

"Cool," he replied.

"Where were you living when this incident occurred?"

"With my girlfriend Linda on Peachtree Run."

"Now earlier, you said something to the officer about school?"

"Yeah, I'm going to school at Delaware Technical Community College."

"How long have you been going there?"

"I don't know, awhile now."

"Before we get started, I have to read your Miranda rights. You have the right to remain silent. Anything you say can and will be used against you in a court of law. You have the right to speak to a lawyer and have him present with you while you're being questioned. If you can't afford to hire a lawyer, one will be appointed to represent you before any questions, if you wish. If you decide to answer any questions, with or without an attorney present, you may stop at any time during the questioning. Do you understand each of these rights as I've explained them to you?"

"Yeah," Damion said.

"Having those rights in mind, do you still wish to talk?"

"Somewhat," he replied.

"You have to say yes or say no. It's your decision."

"Well, yes because I can stop anytime I want, right?"

"Yes," Maher replied.

"So basically, yes, I mean, yeah, I want to talk," Damion hesitantly said.

Detective Maher placed a recording device onto the table and turned it on, capturing every word spoken in the room. "This is Detective Michael Maher of the Delaware State Police. I'm talking to Damion Neal," the detective said as he spoke directly into the device. "Mister Neal, I read you your Miranda rights, correct?"

"Yes," Damion replied.

"And what was your response when I said, 'Do you understand each of these rights?'"

"I understand them."

"And having those rights in mind, do you wish to talk?"

"Yes."

After this exchange, the detective proceeded to ask several questions pertaining to the double homicide which had occurred just five days earlier. "I've been working on this case for a few days now, so there is a lot I already know. Now is your opportunity to tell your side of what happened. Why don't you start on Saturday? What happened Saturday that led you to go over to your ex-girlfriend's house."

"For you to be able to understand everything, I'll have to go back a few days before Saturday."

"Okay. Let's go back further," the detective said.

Detective Maher listened intently to Damion's every word, taking studious notes on a writing pad on the table in front of him. Throughout the course of the interview, Damion seemed incomprehensible at times. His emotional energy was variable and not always consistent with the content of the interview. His thinking appeared impaired, with noted disturbances in thought content. He even had flights of ideas and rapidly, and without prompting, shifted topics as he recounted the incident.

"I need your help. You understand what I'm saying?" Damion stated.

"Uh-huh," the detective replied.

"I need your help because somewhere down the line I'm missing pieces of what happened, you understand?"

The detective paused and said, "I understand how relationships can go. I've been doing this work now for twenty years. I just need you to be honest with me," he said.

"This wasn't supposed to end like this, man. It wasn't," Damion stated.

"I know it wasn't, but..."

"I'm still trying to figure out how all this came about. Still waiting for this nightmare to end. I've been having dreams every night that I'm talking to her."

"Talking to who, Tonessa?" Maher inquired.

"When my friend called my cell phone and said they were dead, I couldn't believe it."

"Who called you?"

"He was like, 'somebody said they're dead—they're out of here.'" Damion paused, then continued, "God is my witness, I could not fucking fathom it, you know what I mean? That's when I said to him, 'You need to check into that again.'"

The inquiry by the detective later shifts to questions about Damion's altercation with Richard outside Tonessa's home on Saturday, November 8. The detective continues to take down notes while listening carefully. "How did the fight between you and Richard begin?"

"On Saturday, I knocked on Tonessa's door and nobody answered. I knocked again and still nobody answered. So then, I called her house phone."

"Uh-huh."

"When I called the house phone, someone answered and then dropped the receiver."

"So, someone was in there?" the detective inquired.

"Right. And that's when I yelled, 'Man, are you in there? Can I get my shit?' I just wanted to get my clothes."

"Uh-huh, and that pissed you off," the detective said as he continued to take notes.

"And that's when I kicked the door in."

"So, they were basically ignoring you?" The detective asked.

"Just let me get my stuff," Damion commented. "You hear me at the door, so what's the problem? It wasn't making sense. None of this is making any goddamn sense."

"So, what happens when you get inside the home?"

Damion explains to the detective that after entering the house, he found Tonessa and Richard sitting on the couch, watching television. He then engaged in a furious argument with Tonessa. "Are you crazy?" she shouted. He reiterated that he just wanted to get his clothes, also questioning why she hadn't answered the door when he knocked. As Damion moved toward a closet near the living room, Richard stood up.

"He gets up off the couch and grabs me like this," Damion said as he demonstrates to the detective. "I was like, 'Hold up. You don't know me like that.' Then he pushed me out the door and we started fighting." Damion recalls.

"Did Tonessa ever hit you or anything like that?"

"No," he said.

"Was she just standing there when you were walking towards the closet?" the detective inquired.

"Yes. But when he pushed me out the door, we all went out the door together."

"How was the fight going? What was going on, did he hit you or did you hit him?" Maher asked.

"No good punches were landing or anything like that, just a lot of tussling. When I pushed him up against the gate, he reversed it, and we landed on the ground together. That's when he took his thumb and stuck that motherfucker in my eye."

"Which eye?" The detective inquired.

"This one right here," Damion said as he pointed to his eye. "The only thing I could think of at that point was that I need to *bite* his ass."

"Uh-huh."

"So, I'm like, 'I gotta bite this motherfucker,' so I bit him on his face."

According to witnesses, the altercation continued for several minutes before it came to an end. There were no serious injuries other than some minor lacerations and bruises.

"We were both exhausted," Damion said.

After about an hour into the interview, Detective Maher began to probe into the details of what happened on Sunday, November 9, the morning Tonessa and Richard were killed.

"What time did you wake up on Sunday morning?" Detective Maher asked.

"Maybe two or three o'clock," Damion responded.

"So, it's really early?"

"Yeah. I don't sleep good anyway."

"And you're at Linda's house when you woke up, right?"

"Yeah."

"Okay. And you don't remember everything that happened?"

Damion paused.

"Damion, you're the only one who can…"

The dam holding back Damion's deepest emotions could no longer withstand the pressure of the interview. The weight of the circumstances broke him down, and he began to sob uncontrollably, almost violently. "I didn't mean it. I didn't even know they got shot. I swear to God I didn't. I was just trying to scare them."

Damion jumped up from his chair, paced back and forth, and cried. He took a moment to collect himself, wiped his tears, and took a deep breath before calming down. He was filled with emotion.

"Sit down, man—sit down," the detective calmly said.

"I swear to God I didn't mean it. I swear," Damion shouted as he began to sob again.

"Tell me—just tell me what happened, man. You're the only one who can tell us what happened," the detective pleaded.

Following his arrest and subsequent charges, the Delaware attorney general sought the death penalty as the punishment in the case. During the week of May 3, 2010, the selection of a death-qualified jury took place in a Dover courthouse, with the trial scheduled to commence on Monday, May 10, 2010.

Approximately half an hour before the opening statements were to be presented to the jury, Damion's attorneys and state prosecutors informed the court clerk of their desire to speak with the judge regarding a one-hour trial delay. Within that hour, Damion's attorney negotiated a deal with the state, resulting in a plea agreement. Damion pleaded guilty to one count of murder in the first degree and one count of murder in the second degree. The state entered a nolle prosequi on the remaining charges, which included two counts of possession of a firearm during the commission of a felony, one count of unauthorized use of a vehicle, one count of harassment, and one count of criminal mischief. The term *nolle prosequi* signifies that Damion would not be charged with those crimes, but the prosecution retained the option to revisit them at a later time, if they chose to do so.

Damion received a life sentence for the first-degree murder of Tonessa and an additional thirty-five-year consecutive sentence for the second-degree murder of Richard. Unless his case is overturned through a legal challenge, Damion will spend the rest of his life in prison. It must have been a difficult decision for him to accept a life sentence, but perhaps it wasn't so difficult. Early in the court proceedings, the prosecutors informed him that they would seek the death penalty if he were found guilty at trial. According to Delaware's legal statute, anyone convicted of a capital crime is subject to a death sentence. So, the prospect of losing his case at trial and facing a lethal injection might have made it easier for him to agree to the plea deal.

On October 7, 2013, Damion's challenge to his conviction was reviewed in the Superior Court of the State of Delaware. His argument was that his attorneys had been ineffective and negligent in representing him. The court ruled on his motion on October 9, 2013, denying Damion relief. This marked his first legal setback in his attempt to overturn his conviction.

Damion did not give up and decided to file an appeal with Delaware's highest court. On April 4, 2014, he submitted another challenge to his conviction, this time filing it in the Supreme Court of the State of Delaware. This petition was based on the denial of his previous filing in the lower Superior Court.

In this instance, a three-justice panel convened in the Supreme Court in Wilmington, Delaware, to review his petition. A few weeks later, the justices rendered their decision, delivering more unwelcome news for Damion. Justice Jacobs authored the opinion for the Supreme Court, affirming the lower court's decision. In their response, the court showed no sympathy for Damion's concerns and stated the following:

"The appellant, Damion Neal, appeals the denial by the Superior Court of his first motion for post-conviction relief. We find no merit in the issues Neal raises on appeal and, accordingly, affirm the Superior Court's judgment."

Damion was dealt yet another defeat in his challenges to his conviction, and unless an extraordinary circumstance should arise, further attempts to challenge his conviction would be extremely unlikely. Initially, it was thought that he might have had the option of filing a habeas corpus petition in the United States Supreme Court, but that turned out to be incorrect. A habeas corpus requires that a person in prison be brought before the court so that the legitimacy of the person's detention can be assessed. There is a statute of limitations for those kinds of petitions, and that time period had expired, barring him from filing in the nation's highest court.

# CHAPTER 8
# WRITING MY WRONGS

IN 2014, LATE-NIGHT TALK SHOW host Jay Leno was fired by NBC and replaced with Jimmy Fallon, who some said was funnier and even more brilliant. That same year, Kanye West and Kim Kardashian were married in Italy and affectionately gained the nickname Kim-Ye, although some people hated it. Beyoncé's younger sister, Solange, was caught on surveillance during an altercation with Jay-Z inside an elevator and everyone thought they had the answers to what happened and why. That same year, Bruno Mars headlined the Super Bowl XLVIII halftime show, and some people said he "rose to the occasion," while critics described his performance as "lackluster." Which brings me to the point that opinions are like *you-know-what*, and everybody has one.

I have faced countless criticisms, more times than I can recall—we all have. If I had heeded my critics, I would have given up a long time ago. What I've learned through my experiences is that when you tune out all the surrounding *noise* and the useless chatter, good things tend to happen.

In 2014, I released my first book, which began as a scary proposition. I was very transparent in my writing, and I wasn't sure how that would be received. I guess that's why after writing the book I shelved it for a while before finally releasing it to the world. It's difficult for a person who has led a compli-

107

cated life to open up knowing the whole world will critique them. You want to talk candidly about your pain, but you also must be a bit cautious. Because of legal reasons, there were some matters I could not write about in detail, and after the book was released, the streets were whispering and so were some of the haters. I knew some people would have a problem with me talking openly about what went on in the streets in those years, but at the end of the day they were the least of my concerns. Anytime you put content out into the public sphere it will open the door for criticism. I went on an emotional rollercoaster to write that piece of literature, and for me that was as personal as it gets. So, I was not going to allow some small-minded peasant to steal that important accomplishment away from me.

To my delight, I received an enormous amount of support from people across the globe, and that was extremely gratifying. From Ireland to the US Virgin Islands, readers were fascinated by my journey. From Boston to New York, Philadelphia, Texas, North Carolina, and Florida, the support I received from readers was overwhelming at times.

I was even invited to Ireland and then to London to have lunch at Piccadilly Circus, where I spoke extensively about what I had written. After returning home from the United Kingdom, I found myself at the Harvard bookstore in Cambridge, Massachusetts, and walking the campus of one of the most prestigious universities in the world where I took pictures in front of the legendary John Harvard statue. Then, I was invited to Johns Hopkins University by Dr. Phil Leaf to speak with students about the new book as well as my life experiences. That same year, I was invited to speak at several colleges and universities across the country. I was also interviewed three times by CNN, as well as multiple times on FOX and the BBC. I had no idea that the issues I wrote about, like poverty, education, substance abuse, and mass incarceration, would resonate with so many people.

I heard from a woman in Anchorage, Alaska, who reached out to me through Facebook. Her son was incarcerated for selling illegal narcotics. She said that she read my book and wanted to know if I could mail her son a free copy at the prison where he was serving time. At first I was skeptical because I did not believe, at the time, that there were any Black women living in frigid Anchorage, Alaska, but sure enough there were. I know it sounds ridiculous, but it's the truth! So, a few days later, I went to the post office and sent an autographed copy of my first book to Alaska, the state known as *the Last Frontier*.

I found it comforting to connect with so many people who could relate to my message. Immediately, I discovered that I loved being an author. Writing felt good in a way that nothing else did. Through writing I became a better human being, a better father, a better man, a better citizen: a better everything. Writing was the mechanism I used to help take this giant leap into a stratosphere where you're free to be whomever you want without the fear of judgement. The grueling journey to get there was well worth it, and it helped me discover who I really was.

A few weeks after returning from the United Kingdom, I received a telephone call from a close friend after she read my book. She was not the type of person to talk much about issues within her family, but my writing had sparked something in her.

"Hello Kevin, its Erinn," she said.

"Hey, what's up?"

"I'm just leaving my office headed home. I'm feeling a little down today. I just read your book and it brought tears to my eyes."

"Really? Which chapter? Which part?" I asked.

"When you were talking about your dad being an alcoholic. That was painful to read. I could relate so much because my father was an alcoholic too. Reading that opened up some old wounds."

I was humbled by conversations like these with readers because initially, I had no idea that my story would touch so many hearts and minds. I believe that it was the fact that I'd written the story as authentically as possible that moved them. The real story that you cry about when the lights are out. We often camouflage our truth and cover up our pain with expensive Louis Vuitton bags imported from Paris or five-hundred-dollar jeans made with custom stitching because, like Kanye West said, *"they made us hate ourself and love their wealth."*

Some of us may even drink expensive bottles of vodka to drown our pain or smoke hookah that may contain toxic ingredients. We cover up our pain like it doesn't exist or like it's not there at all until something comes along to force that suppressed trauma to the surface. Maybe it's the relationship with an abusive partner that you've endured for years, or maybe it's the absence of a parent in our lives. Maybe you grew up in poverty, and the guilt of now being able to live up to the status quo hurts. Maybe you were sexually abused as a child, and it left a mark of devastation that you conceal from the world. Everyone has pain, and their pain may be different from the pain you endured, but it's still pain and it's still important to them.

At first, I couldn't believe I'd completed the grueling task of writing an entire book. I remember getting questions from people like, "Did you write it on your own?" or, "You didn't use real names, did you?" I had become a master at telling the story the way it was and not the watered-down version of it. I needed to let people know that there are no friends in the drug business, and it is not as glamorous as people may think it is.

Yes, I took some flak from some wannabe critics, but I stood by every word. It was an awkward experience for the once laidback guy who voluntarily entered the lion's den of public opinion. And if I had a chance to do it all over again, I would not change a thing.

When the book was being edited, I remember being confronted with a serious challenge. My editor was diagnosed with prostate cancer. His name was Gregory Kane, and he was a former writer for the *Baltimore Sun* newspaper. After the newspaper began to downsize, he was offered a buyout and he retired, which gave him more time to work with me. He was one of the kindest, strongest, and most brilliant Black men I had ever met. When he told me that he had been diagnosed with cancer I was very concerned, but he seemed not to be.

"My doctors have everything under control. I'm going to kick the shit out of this freaking disease," Gregory said.

Hearing those words from a man that I had grown fond of while on this journey made me feel proud to know him and gave me even more courage and confidence to push ahead. During the times when I was apprehensive about telling my story or days when I was concerned about what people would think, Gregory would say to me, "Don't worry about them. Just be honest in your writing." I also remember him saying, "Write until your hand falls off and if it does, learn how to write with the other hand." That's when I realized that if this man can fight cancer, I can surely write a bunch of words down on a piece of paper.

But just one month before the book was scheduled to be released, I was home scrolling through social media and saw a post that Gregory had died. Immediately, I called his cell phone but there was no answer. Then, I did some research online where I found the official announcement from the *Baltimore Sun* newspaper stating that Gregory Kane had passed after a long bout with cancer. It was surreal because I had just communicated with him a few weeks earlier via email and he had seemed upbeat.

A few months after Gregory's passing, I was invited to Dallas, Texas, by the United States Conference of Mayors to speak at their Eighty-Second Annual Summer Meeting. It was a gathering of three hundred mayors from cities all across the country there to promote urban policy and to create a forum in which to share ideas. One of the high-level officials at the USCM, Crystal Swann, read my book and asked me to speak at the conference about the impact of heroin and opioids on communities across America. It was a topic that I had written about in the book and one about which I knew far more than I should have.

"I want you to help the USCM further educate these leaders on this epidemic that's sweeping the nation." Crystal said.

I never thought in a million years that someone would send me a special invitation, and even pay me, to talk about some of the nefarious activities I had been involved with in the past. A friend of mine told me that today I'm what's considered a *subject matter expert.* I guess if you want to learn a little bit about the moon it wouldn't hurt to talk to an astronaut who has been there.

After arriving at the airport in Dallas, I took a taxi downtown to the luxurious Hyatt Regency Hotel. When I first walked inside the hotel lobby, I was impressed with its style and elegance. It's a relief when you've been traveling all day and arrive at a place of comfort where you can rest and unwind. After I checked in at the front desk, I grabbed my bags, took the elevator up to my room, and got comfortable. My hotel room was large but cozy and it had all the amenities a weary traveler would appreciate.

As I looked out of my seventeenth-floor window onto the city skyline, the skies were cloudy and yet it was still ninety-two degrees outside. A thunderstorm was trying to roll in, but the Texas skies were fighting back the challenge.

After a short nap, I whipped out my laptop, connected to wi-fi, turned on some music, ripped open a box of Oreo cookies, and started working. I was still editing my presentation for the conference, and I was a little anxious. I wanted to do a good job and I wanted to impress the conference attendees.

While I was typing away on my computer and putting the final touches on my presentation, I became hungry, so I ordered dinner. About thirty minutes later, room service was knocking on the door, and I opened it as fast as I could.

"Good evening, sir."

"Come in," I said.

"I hope you're enjoying your evening here at the Hyatt," the waiter said as he rolled in the cart full of appetizing dishes.

He was a short-statured Mexican gentleman who stood about 5'4" tall. Several years ago, I had a Mexican friend named Jesus who looked exactly like him. It was like I was looking at his twin.

"You have roasted chicken, asparagus, and garlic mashed potatoes. And also, a glass of cranberry juice with no ice," he said.

"Thanks. How much?"

The waiter handed me the bill inside a black leather booklet. *Not bad*, I thought as I placed two twenty-dollar bills inside.

"I'll be back with your change, sir."

"Don't worry about it," I said.

"Thank you, sir. Have a great evening." Then, he left and closed the door behind him.

I swear, I thought I was losing my mind that day because Jesus and the waiter could have been identical twins. Jesus had been the name of my contact down in Puebla, Mexico, who set me up with an undercover DEA agent several years ago. I had been in Laredo, Texas, a town close to the border, putting together a deal to buy ten kilos. That was the last time I had been in the Lone Star State and shortly thereafter, I was arrested.

Ironically, Jesus unwittingly saved my life. At the time I was arrested I thought it was the worst thing that could have ever happened, but in hindsight it was the best thing that could've happened. The result of his actions removed me from a world where something even worse could have occurred, like getting killed. Getting arrested is how I ended up in Allenwood where I started down a path that I had never thought possible. Allenwood is the place where I reassessed a life headed towards destruction. And now, I was back in Texas putting together an even bigger deal: a deal to help save the lives of children across America from the disease of addiction.

I had been travelling most of the day, so my plan was to get a good night's sleep, recharge, and be rejuvenated in the morning. But instead of resting, I was up half the night working on my presentation. I slept only four hours, and the next thing I knew it was six o'clock in the morning and my editing was still not complete. That's when I came up with the silly idea of drinking two cans of Red Bull on an empty stomach. Within fifteen minutes I was so hyper I felt like I had consumed ten cups of black coffee.

On June 22, 2014, I addressed a room full of mayors from across the country who were curious to hear what the former drug dealer had to say. I was one of five guest panelists, including Michael Botticelli, acting director of the White House Office on National Drug Control Policy; Ronald Davis, US Department of Justice; Mayor Martin Walsh from the city of Boston; and Mayor Ashley Swearengin from the city of Fresno, California. The topic for our panel was titled "Heroin Epidemic in America," which was a priority for every elected official in the room. The Red Bull I had been sipping for the last few hours was still going strong when I began to address the audience.

"Good morning, ladies, and gentlemen. I began dealing drugs at age sixteen, and by twenty-three I was making twenty thousand dollars a day. There was a time when I was involved with selling drugs to people suffering from the disease of addiction, but for the last few years I have been working tirelessly with a nonprofit organization to educate the world on the dangers of illegal narcotics."

Then I said:

"If there were a way to enhance the likelihood that our children could steer clear of accidents, injuries, a variety of health issues, and even premature mortality, while also performing better academically and thriving in their careers, would we seize that opportunity?"

The silence in the room was deafening and you could hear a pin drop on the floor.

"The impact of substance abuse, involving both drugs and alcohol, inflicts profound harm on individuals and has incurred immense economic costs for families, businesses, and our government, potentially reaching into the trillions of dollars. After decades of an unsuccessful 'war on drugs,' it has become evident that addressing our society's struggle with substance use demands a long-term, multifaceted strategy. This approach necessitates the active involvement of various stakeholders, including civic leaders, government agencies, corporations, community and faith-based organizations, philanthropic entities, educational institutions, not-for-profit youth service organizations, parents, and, notably, young people themselves."

I went on to tell the audience that there was a tremendous amount of data confirming that doctors in the United States prescribe enough painkillers to medicate everyone in the country twenty-four hours a day for an entire month. And

I watched as their mouths dropped. Most of them were surprised, and there were some who seemed a bit skeptical, but there was plenty of data to support my claim. Heroin addiction was already flooding the country, but once prescription drug abuse skyrocketed, it turned into a tidal wave. It was no longer just a problem in urban America, but it had become a disaster for white kids living in the suburbs. And the term *War on Drugs* was no longer being used by pundits and politicians when discussing the issue. Now that it was taking a toll on suburbanites and rural America it was being described as a *Public Health Crisis*, and addicts were no longer being vilified like they had been in the past.

"In closing I would like to say: the opioid problem in America is real. Right now, we need grade-level prevention education in our schools. But we also need to educate doctors on ways to identify addicted individuals looking to manipulate the system to get prescription drugs they really don't need. Thank you."

At the end of my presentation, I received a round of applause. I was tired and ready to leave, but then, several of the mayors and their staff came over to congratulate me and to take down my contact information. They wanted to invite me to speak to youth organizations in their cities to help create even more awareness.

Former US congressman and mayor of Oakland, California, Ron Dellums also came over to congratulate me after I delivered my speech. Crystal Swann had introduced me to the former congressman months earlier, and he had become a man I both respected and admired for his integrity and honor. He was also someone I considered a mentor and friend. Prior to the conference, we had been meeting privately in Washington, DC, and he played a significant role in my growth and development as an activist.

"Man, let me tell you something. You did great! I've never heard you speak like that before," the former congressman said.

"Thanks, Ron. I appreciate that."

I was thankful for this incredible opportunity to be there in the room with so many influential people, but the Red Bull was starting to wear off. All I wanted to do at this point was go back to my hotel room and get some sleep.

In late 2014, I was asked by my friend Monique Dixon, who worked with the NAACP Legal Defense Fund in Washington, DC, to join the planning committee for President Barack Obama's Clemency Project. The Clemency Project was an initiative where nonviolent drug offenders serving time in federal prison petitioned the White House to have their prison sentences commuted, or reduced, by the president. I was assigned to a workgroup tasked with developing resources for inmates being released under the program. Under this initiative 1,700 federal prisoners were either released from prison or had their sentences drastically reduced. While I was involved in the project, I pushed hard to make mental health resources available to people being released under the program. I remember getting into a heated exchange on a conference call with a Federal Bureau of Prisons official over the issue of increasing mental health access for the prisoners who were getting out. Many of them had been incarcerated for decades. The gentleman didn't understand why I was advocating so much for increased access to counseling and treatment for formerly incarcerated individuals. It was work that for obvious reasons, I took very personally—and work that I will forever be proud of.

Becoming an author forced me to look at the world through a different frame of reference. And it was that different frame of reference that moved me to become a community activist. That was the same year an unarmed eighteen-year-old Black man named Michael Brown was shot and killed by police in Ferguson, Missouri, and rioting erupted. It was also just two years removed from the murder of sixteen-year-old Trayvon Martin in Sanford, Florida. People wanted to know what my opinion was regarding the issue of police brutality in America. So, I used my platform to make as many thoughtful and informative comments as I could with the hope that my words would force them and others to think deeper or go out and conduct their own research. One day, a woman said to me, "We wouldn't need a *Black Lives Matter* movement if we didn't have three hundred years of *Black Lives Never Mattered.*" And that was one of the few times when I had no response.

I remember receiving a phone call from my former girl-friend, the one who broke up with me while I was writing my first book. The one who told me that I was boring and that I was "spending too much time writing."

"Hey, I just saw you on CNN news and I'm so proud of you," she said.

"Thanks, Takiyah."

"I've always believed in you and your work." she continued.

"Really?"

"Of course. That's why I've always been so supportive."

After hearing these outrageous comments from my former girlfriend, I remember thinking, *How do you even respond to nonsense like this?* Then I began thinking, *Dumping me was probably the best thing that could have ever happened.*

One day, my friend Mario Barrett, a superstar R&B singer and a Baltimore native, approached me with an important proposal that I couldn't refuse.

"I need to do something to help these kids, and I need your help," Mario said.

Mario skyrocketed to stardom in the early 2000s with his eponymous debut album, titled *Mario*, featuring chart-top-ping tracks like "Just a Friend" and "Braid My Hair." His smooth R&B vocals earned widespread acclaim, establishing him as a prominent figure in the music industry during that era. Over the years, he built an impressive discography, including albums like *Turning Point* and *Go*, among others. Some of his unforgettable hit records include "Let Me Love You," "How Do I Breathe," and "Crying Out for Me."

In addition to his flourishing music career, Mario ventured into the world of acting, appearing in films such as *Step Up*, *Freedom Writers*, and later in the hit television series *Empire*.

I vividly recall sitting in Mario's Baltimore penthouse when a special delivery arrived via FedEx. It was a package from Harpo Films, the company owned by none other than Oprah Winfrey. Inside, we found a movie script for a film titled *The Great Debaters*, starring Denzel Washington and Nate Parker. The script had been sent to Mario to prepare for an upcoming audition in Hollywood. As I read the script, I couldn't help but think, *Damn, this guy really is a star.*

Mario and I had both grown up with addicted parents— his mother struggled with heroin addiction, and my father battled chronic alcoholism. These shared experiences led to many heartfelt conversations about the impact of parental addiction on children. It was eye opening at the time, and these were conversation that I rarely had with others. And from this we developed a close bond.

"I want to do something that really matters," Mario said.

"Like what?" I asked.

"Start a charity," he replied.

"What kind of charity?" I said.

"Something to keep kids away from these fucking drugs," he said.

Mario already had a nonprofit organization with a focus on children, but it was being managed by his former manager and individuals connected to the music industry. Due to his deep concern for the issue of addiction, he was dissatisfied with the way they were operating the charity.

After several discussions and some consulting on the issue of drug prevention education, we decided to take action and start a charity to help children facing challenges similar to those we faced when we were growing up. Soon afterwards, we filed paperwork with the state of Maryland to establish a nonprofit organization dedicated to supporting children of addicted parents, known as COAP. We named the nonprofit "The Do Right Foundation."

In no time, we assembled a board of directors consisting of lawyers, businessmen, accountants, and public health professionals. A real estate developer named Pat Turner joined the board and granted us permission to conduct board meeting in Silo Point, a luxury condominium development he owned. This period was a turning point for me—an opportunity for redemption and a chance to make a meaningful difference in the world. Shelonda Stokes, who founded a media and entertainment firm, helped us build a very important relationship with former mayor Stephanie Rawlings-Blake. Two of my other great friends, Guy and Nupur Flynn, joined the board and their leadership as well as guidance turned out to be invaluable. A lot of very influential people were very enthusiastic about supporting us.

At the time, Mario was a celebrity who garnered the attention of thousands of young people around the world. We believed that using his platform to raise awareness about substance abuse prevention and making positive life choices was a good strategy to build a sustainable charity.

Mario and I were like brothers, and though we sometimes had our disagreements, we were a formidable duo, and we accomplished a lot together. Our efforts even garnered the attention of the White House and the National Institute of Health. In 2012, we were invited to Columbus, Ohio, where we addressed five thousand students on the campus of Ohio State University at the height of the opioid epidemic in America. It was a very inspiring moment for both of us. Working with professionals who understood substance use disorder and mental health from a clinical perspective was incredibly gratifying and provided me with a different perspective on these critical issues.

After this experience I had been swept up in for years started to subside, I began to reflect. Talking about my pain during speaking engagements, book signings, interviews, or even one-on-one conversations was therapeutic in ways that are still hard to describe. There was no doubt in my mind that I had been adversely affected by traumatic events that had occurred many years earlier and I was still struggling to cope with them. Sometimes I would get choked up just talking about them, and other times the palms of my hands would get sweaty, and I would feel extremely anxious.

But, overall, this experience was very gratifying in several ways. I discovered that as a writer it's not always about you, but it's about the number of people you resonate with. How many people can you make laugh, smile, or cry with just words printed on a piece of paper? How many people can you challenge to think deeper so that they can discover a bit more about what's inside of themselves? So, this incredible journey, where I used meaningful phrases and sentences to reach the masses and where I created a piece of literature that they could feel and not just read, may shed some light on the *why* of the rest of this story. Why did a murder trial in Delaware and the issue of mental health move me into action the way that it did?

# CHAPTER 9

# MURDER HE WROTE

ON THE MORNING OF DECEMBER 12, 2016, it was cold, blustery, and rainy. The sky was roaring, and Mother Nature was angry. The sound of raindrops tapping against my bedroom window was annoying, but it served as a wakeup call. As I tried to get out of bed, I struggled. When I rolled over, my body felt achy, and I was a bit groggy. Then, I realized I had had another rough night of sleep, full of twisted and deranged villains chasing me with knives. The mental scars I acquired many years ago had returned in the form of more nightmares. I had hoped that the torment from the past was still idle deep down in my psyche, but I was wrong. It was confusing sometimes because one night my dreams were pleasant and filled with images of supermodels on white sand beaches, and the next night they were scenes from *Nightmare on Elm Street*. In this latest episode, Freddy Krueger was chasing me through an alley with a twelve-inch blade.

I was in a mental quagmire that morning and struggled to get the day started. I had to be in the shower, dressed, and out of the house by nine o'clock. It was an important day because I was headed north to Delaware to learn more about Damion's case. The amateur journalist in me had taken over my life, and I needed to understand more about what had happened in General's Greene.

Just a few months earlier, the Department of Justice for the State of Delaware had granted me permission to interview the prosecutor in Damion's murder case. The prosecutor's name was Susan Schmidhauser, and she was one of the two state's attorneys responsible for convicting him. Ironically, she was a native of the Baltimore metropolitan area who had relocated to Delaware to practice law. So, a Baltimore native would be meeting with a Baltimore native, to discuss the terrible predicament of another Baltimore native, all inside the small town of Dover.

The prearranged meeting with Mrs. Schmidhauser was scheduled for 11:00 a.m. at the Dover Department of Justice offices on Water Street. I had spoken with her briefly by phone a few months earlier, but during our upcoming face-to-face meeting there would be an opportunity to have a more in-depth discussion. I was surprised that the state agreed to speak with me about the high-profile murder case, but nevertheless I was grateful.

It was 8:45 a.m. when I left home for the drive to Delaware, and the angry skies were beginning to clear. The day had begun to evolve into another typical autumn day in the mid-Atlantic. Traffic was light and according to Google Maps the drive north on Interstate 95 would take just under two hours.

As I drove north on the interstate, my thoughts were primarily on the upcoming meeting. While en route, I decided to stop at a public rest area about thirty minutes south of the Maryland-Delaware state line. The first thing I noticed when I walked inside was the bright orange and lavender Dunkin Donuts sign that lit up the place like a Christmas tree. Within seconds I recognized the smell of heaven in the form of fresh-baked donuts and pastries. I thought about ordering a large latte, but after some consideration, I concluded that my lactose-intolerant digestive tract was in no mood for trouble. On the other hand, two freshly toasted coconut donuts and a cold bottle of apple juice would do the trick.

Shortly before eleven o'clock, I arrived in the city of Dover, and it looked exactly like I imagined it would. It was a quiet enclave that had the feel of conservative middle America. When I travel to different cities, I appreciate learning small pieces of history about my destination. It helps me get a feel for the people who live there. After some research, I learned that Dover had a population of approximately thirty-seven thousand residents. It's the capital and the second largest city in the state, in a region affectionately called the Delmarva. It is also one of the oldest cities in the US which dates all the way back before the American Revolution. Before I began looking into Damion's case, I did not know much about Dover, so my knowledge of the city was minimal, but there was one thing that stood out to me. In 2008, there had been a total of four homicides in the city of Dover, and Damion was responsible for fifty percent of all the murders committed there that year.

Within a few minutes of exiting the interstate, I arrived at the nondescript three-story office building on Water Street, which fit nicely into the surrounding community. After parking, I grabbed my laptop out of the trunk and walked over to the smoked-glass front doors of the building. After I made my way onto the second floor, I informed the receptionist at the desk that I was there for an interview.

"I'm here to meet with Carl Kanefsky and Susan Schmidhauser," I said to the woman sitting behind the bulletproof glass.

"Please have a seat, Mister Shird. I'll notify them that you've arrived."

A few minutes later, Carl Kanefsky walked into the reception area to greet me. He was a tall middle-aged white man dressed like you would expect someone from the prosecutor's office to be dressed. Kanefsky was assigned to Wilmington, which was about forty-five minutes from Dover. But since he helped clear and schedule the interview, he agreed to be at the Dover office to facilitate the meeting.

"How are you, Mister Shird? Great to finally meet you."

I had spoken to him on the phone several times. For months, he tried to arrange the interview, but everyone had conflicting schedules. It took a while to coordinate, but eventually he was able to get confirmation from his supervisor. In the beginning, I did not know what to expect from him or anyone from his office because this was the first time that I had ever dealt with criminal prosecutors in that fashion.

"It's good to meet you, too," I said.

"How was the drive up?"

"It wasn't bad."

"Which route did you take? Did you come over the Chesapeake Bay Bridge?"

"I actually drove up Interstate 95 to DE-7 and then DE-1. My GPS guided me the entire way."

While I was speaking with Kanefsky, the prosecutor from Damion's case walked into the lobby.

"I'm Mrs. Schmidhauser."

"How are you doing?" I asked.

"I'm doing well. We can get started whenever you're ready," she said.

From the second-floor lobby, I was escorted down the long hallway to a drab conference room with no windows. It was the place where seasoned prosecutors conducted the business of prosecuting criminal defendants for all sorts of crimes. The room was dim and ominous, and I could not stop wondering if it was the same room where Damion may have been interrogated.

Before we began, I explained that I was using a dictation app on my iPhone to record our interview.

"Okay, no problem," Mrs. Schmidhauser replied.

I began our discussion in a bland way just to break the ice. I already had a lot of information about Damion's case from court documents and media reports, but there were still several gaps I needed to fill.

"Where were you when you were first informed of the murders at General's Greene?" I asked.

"It was the day after the homicides, and I was here in the office."

"In 2008, there were four murders here in Dover. What was your immediate reaction to the level of violence in this case?" I asked.

"A double homicide, at that time, in Kent County, was unheard of and sad. I'm sure there have been others, but none come to mind. This was also a tough situation for the families of both victims. We had a job to do, and we did it, but this was terrible. By the time I got wind of the incident the detectives had a suspect in custody. The investigation developed quickly, but that's not strange in Kent County. At that time most of our homicides were solved rather fast."

Next, I asked her if she remembered the community's reaction to the incident. She responded by saying that she did not remember there being a large public outcry, but that many of the people in the community were very concerned about the level of violence.

At the beginning of the interview, I still was not 100 percent sure as to why Damion committed the crimes. He just did not seem like a guy who would kill for love, but that was the hypothesis that had been drawn by detectives. Ironically, I still remembered the statement he made when we were in the county jail six years before this incident occurred when he said, "I hope nothing like that happens while I'm in here. I would kill my daughter's mother."

The prosecutor said that for two to three years, prior to her death, Tonessa and Damion had an on-again-and-off-again sexual relationship. The day before the homicides, Damion came to Tonessa's home, kicked in her front door, and got into a physical altercation with Richard. Richard and Tonessa had just entered into a new relationship. During the fight Damion bit Richard in the face, so there were warrants pending for his arrest. Because the police could not find him, he was not arrested on the misdemeanor assault charge. Based on those facts, she believed that Damion was upset about Tonessa's relationship with Richard.

"So, the fight involving Richard happened one day before the murders?" I asked.

"Yes. The altercation occurred primarily because Tonessa was not returning Damion's phone calls. She was ignoring him because she was at home with Richard. Damion was upset, so he went to her house and banged on the door, but no one would answer. So, he kicked it in. Damion and Tonessa got into an intense argument, and then ultimately, there were witnesses who observed Damion and Richard in a physical fight outside the home."

"Had you prosecuted a double murder before?" I asked.

"For more than six years, I prosecuted sexual assaults of small children. A double murder is certainly a heinous crime. Is it more heinous than sexually assaulting a child? I do not know. Both crimes have a tremendous impact on families: an impact that lasts forever."

Prosecutors had an enormous amount of evidence and witnesses against Damion. For instance, after his fight with Richard, Damion met with friends, with whom he discussed the altercation. Linda, Damion's girlfriend at the time, reported to the police that he was severely intoxicated and that she brought him home, tucked him into bed, and he went to sleep. She also reported that when she went to wake him up the next morning, Damion was not there. The keys to her vehicle were gone, and the gun that she owned was also missing.

"A state identification card belonging to Neal was found by a neighbor who was out walking their dog. His girlfriend reported to detectives that she tried to call him several times when she woke up and eventually spoke to him. Even after pressing him, he would not tell her where he was. She said something to the effect of, 'Where are you and where is my car?'" The prosecutor said.

"Was a murder weapon ever recovered?" I asked.

"I believe he reported to the police that he threw the gun off the Chesapeake Bay Bridge on his way to Baltimore, but I can't be certain," she said.

Then I asked her if she knew why Damion returned to Baltimore after the murders.

"I don't know for sure, but I guess it was because that's where he had family, and he definitely couldn't stay in Dover because two people were dead. Based on the timeline we developed, soon after the murders he drove down to Baltimore."

"Was there any forensic evidence that linked Damion to the crime?"

"No. Not to my knowledge," she said.

Then, I asked her if she thought there was anything in his background indicating that he could be capable of such a terrible act.

"Any person who doesn't want their significant other with someone else is capable of committing such a crime," she said. "There was nothing specific about his background, but there's nothing specific about most people's background in a domestic violence homicide case."

Personally, I disagree with that assumption because from my research, oftentimes in domestic violence cases there is a history of physical abuse. But the nagging question that I still could not answer was what had brought Damion to Dover in the first place. His family lived in Baltimore, and when we were in Allenwood he never mentioned Delaware. "I have no idea what brought him here." She answered. "Was this the first death-penalty case you've prosecuted?" "Yes."

Mrs. Schmidhauser explained that this was a death-penalty-eligible case, which was resolved by a plea agreement the morning the trial was supposed to begin. Damion's defense team approached her and her co-prosecutor and inquired about whether they would accept a plea deal. There were conversations about who would be the person that could give the authorization for a plea which had to go up the chain of command in her office. She went on to explain that, because there is a process of how murder cases can be resolved, it was a requirement that her supervisor get involved in the matter.

"Homicide cases are important, and the administration plays an active role with the assigned prosecutors in whether a plea will be offered and whether we can accept a plea," she said.

When asked about Damion's mental health she said that Damion's attorney mentioned that his mental state was deteriorating at the time of the murders, but that she was not surprised they explored that defense. I was curious as to whether that was a factor for the prosecution in considering a plea agreement.

"No, because to our knowledge, there was no information like that revealed during the investigation," she said.

She went on to explain that Damion was not someone that they had information about who had schizophrenia or some other documented mental health illness where he was receiving treatment or had family members who could confirm that he was deteriorating. She said that he also was not someone who had just stopped taking prescribed medication and prior to committing the crime he began to deteriorate. She also stated that it is common for some defendants, either after they are arrested, or after they have pled guilty to a crime, to say, "My mental health was an issue." She said that she is never surprised to hear that type of defense, but her reaction to that is always, "Well, where's the proof?" She said there was a homicide case in the past where someone had a well-documented mental health issue, and she knew from day one that their mental health status, or chronic condition, might have played a role in the defendant committing the crime, but that wasn't her experience with Damion.

"Were you surprised when you were approached by his attorney about a plea bargain?" I asked.

She responded by saying that defendants facing a life sentence, whether that's because of their habitual-offender status, or because it's a murder case, and they're likely to be sentenced to life anyway, that it's no surprise when they elect to go to trial, because what do they have to lose? They're going to get the same sentence whether they accept a plea or go to trial. In Damion's case, it was not necessarily the same, because he was proceeding with a death-penalty-eligible trial. But by taking a plea deal he knew that he was going to get a life sentence and that the court would not be deciding whether he would be put to death or not.

Mrs. Schmidhauser said she did not remember a lot about the two victims' families but went on to say that in this case and in a lot of cases, the conversation that she has with families is that a plea bargain is difficult to overturn. It provides finality because the mandatory life sentence in Delaware is life with no parole. It is not necessarily life in other states. If the state were to go to trial, and they were successful, the death penalty is the ultimate sentence, but there will be years of appeals by the defendant.

"Do you remember how the family was coping after the case was resolved?" I asked.

"Prosecutors often do not have a lot of contact with families after a case is closed. Some State's Attorney offices have social workers who connect families with resources like mental health services if they need ongoing counseling. Unless a victim's family member calls a prosecutor, we will not have contact with them because normally after the day of sentencing, we part ways," she said.

Surprisingly, she went on to say that this case provided a considerable amount of education for the people who work in her office.

"There was a question that if he had been arrested on Saturday night when the warrants were issued, would that have made a difference? My first reaction was no because it was a misdemeanor warrant, and the likelihood of the court releasing him on bail was possible," she said. "The court probably would not have held him on a misdemeanor assault, but after the murders, there were a lot of conversations about increased efforts that could have been made to find him. When there's an active domestic violence warrant, there should be more effort to get that person into custody, immediately. But in his case, I'm not sure if that would have made a difference because even if they had arrested him at midnight, he could have been out in a couple of hours, and the same events could have unfolded."

I had a list of twenty-five questions that I intended to ask the prosecutor, but many of her answers prompted me to ask follow-up questions that took up a lot more time. This case had more twists and turns than I would have imagined.

I explained to Mrs. Schmidhauser that while I was reviewing court records, I discovered that the judge ordered a psychological evaluation, and that I had tried to get the document from the court clerk but was told the record was sealed.

"The court seals all mental health records," she said. "The public doesn't have the right to look at the mental health history of a defendant, so it's not available for public consumption."

She went on to say that there was conversation about whether or not Damion was going to present an extreme emotional distress (EED) defense at trial and that it was the state's position that his case was not an EED case. EED is a legal defense available to defendants in some murder cases. It suggests that a defendant was not in their right frame of mind when the crime occurred and was triggered by an extraordinary amount of emotional stress.

"Extreme emotional distress requires more of an immediate reaction," she said. "An example of an EED defense is: you come home and open your bedroom door, and you find your wife in bed with somebody else. As a result, you shoot and kill them. That's an immediate response to a traumatic event. The State's position was that Neal's case did not fit that definition because several hours had gone by, and a lot of intervening events had occurred. He went out drinking with friends and then he was taken home and put to bed by his girlfriend. He slept for a few hours before waking up and making a conscious decision to steal a gun, steal a car, and go back to Tonessa's house. It was not like, 'I just found out she was dating someone else, and now I'm going to choke her to death.' Initially, his attorneys pursued extreme emotional distress as a defense, which is why there was a psychological evaluation ordered by the judge."

During my drive back to Baltimore, I replayed the conversation with the prosecutor over and over in my head. I was on a fact-finding mission, and I learned things of which I had previously been unaware. It had been clear to me, for years, that Damion was the shooter, but I noticed that my assertion to the prosecutor that he could have been dealing with mental health issues at the time was oddly met with some resistance. I was not trying to develop a defense for him, I was just probing, but it seemed as if I may have encroached on a sensitive topic.

On the drive home, I thought a lot about the victims in the case, especially Richard. According to the prosecutor Richard had been released from prison just two days before he was killed. He was released on Friday and by Sunday morning, he was dead. You could argue that Richard just happened to be in the wrong place at the wrong time. This was my first time learning this piece of information, and it was shocking. Before meeting with the prosecutor, I had almost no information as to when Richard entered into Tonessa's life, and now I felt terrible for the guy. Even though he was in a fight with Damion on Saturday, there is a high probability that he never saw any of this coming. Less than forty-eight hours before his death he was walking out of a prison cell making plans for the future and not making plans for a funeral.

After the meeting in Dover, I was more eager to understand why Damion made the decision that night to leave his girlfriend's house, drive to his ex-girlfriend's house, where he had already damaged the front door, and commit a double homicide. According to the police, after his fight with Richard, Tonessa and Damion spoke briefly on the phone, so he knew that law enforcement officials were looking for him, and he had to know that if Tonessa was harmed in any way, he would be the prime suspect.

The prosecutor stated that Damion had been drinking heavily just hours before the murders. So, another question I had was, if he had lost at trial and the prosecutors had pursued the death penalty, how much of a factor would those details have played at sentencing? Also, how much of Damion's mental health history had the state really assessed?

I have never been a proponent of the use of the death penalty in America's criminal justice system. We have seen far too many mishaps in cases where defendants were wrongly convicted of crimes through negligence as well as corruption, and some of those defendants were either executed or came very close to it. The death penalty is not an exact science, but it must be, if we are going to allow states to apply it.

I had some concerns about the prosecutor's pursuit of the death penalty, but the more I reviewed the documents related to the case, the more I realized how troubling the case was. There was an overwhelming amount of evidence against Damion, so I understood why his lawyers cut a deal. There was a good chance that he was headed to the death chamber, where he would have received an injection of pentobarbital, pancuronium bromide, and potassium chloride, the same deadly combination of drugs used to end the life of John Allen Muhammad, the infamous DC Sniper.

## CHAPTER 10

# HURT PEOPLE HURT PEOPLE

*"I'M GOING TO KILL HIM one day. I don't like this sucker. I'm not sure why, I just don't. Matter of fact, I might get rid of him tonight."*

Most of the time, this type of jargon is unalarming to those of us who are used to hearing it in the street. After years of consuming these kinds of statements, we become desensitized to them. Someone may even say something like, "Don't worry. He's upset right now, but he'll calm down." Most of the time, the source of this anger is never fully understood, not even by the orator himself. But sometimes, these situations escalate, and when they do, they have the potential to turn deadly.

For most people, committing murder isn't easy, especially when it's premeditated and there's ample time to reconsider. I've been in that position before, standing there, furious, with my finger on the trigger, but I couldn't bring myself to kill someone in cold blood. Frankly, I didn't have it in me. Would I battle tooth and nail to defend myself? Absolutely. But that is as far as I would ever want to go.

A short time after meeting with the prosecutor in Damion's case, I reached out to a good friend and associate to learn more about mental health as it relates to violence. Her name is Terrie M. Williams, and she is a bestselling author and literary agent. I first met Terrie back in 2014 through my friend and bestselling author Wes Moore who is now the governor of the state of Maryland. Terrie was very close to famed writer and scholar Maya Angelou, and she also represented comedians Eddie Murphy and Bill Cosby for a time. Terrie filled a void in my life that was left after Gregory Kane died of prostate cancer. Terrie gave me great advice on writing and introduced me to many of the important players in the world of literature. Besides being an author and speaker, Terrie is also a licensed clinical social worker. In 2008, she released her bestselling book titled *Black Pain: It Just Looks Like We're Not Hurting*, which examines unaddressed mental and emotional illness. Terrie once suffered what was described as a severe bout with depression and was forced to put her career on hold while she recovered. In an *Essence* magazine interview titled "Depression and the Superwoman," she speaks candidly about the issue. She specifically drew attention to the reluctance of people who won't seek treatment due to social stigmas and a variety of other culturally specific issues.

"I used to lecture at colleges and churches across the country to encourage people to come forward and discuss their own struggles. The goal was to use my position to break a taboo that had rendered mental health illness unacceptable and invisible," Terry said.

In her book, *Black Pain*, she writes candidly about her challenges and her journey to help others. "For years, I was afraid to show my pain because I believed what so many of us believe: that I am the only one feeling such deep pain, the only one who has secrets, shame, and insecurities, that people who show their pain can't handle their business, and that it's okay to feel low for a day or two, but after that you should just 'snap' out of it."

Terrie motivated me to want to learn even more about my own struggles and what I could do to help myself.

"You mentioned that you have terrible nightmares and don't sleep well at night and haven't for several years, right?" she asked.

"Yes," I replied.

"Well, that's not good because when a person cannot sleep at night, they are not getting enough important rest, so physically the body is not working at one hundred percent, because it cannot. When this happens, the body suffers, and this can result in serious health problems like heart disease, high blood pressure, and lowered immune system responses. These are just some of the things the body experiences when you are not sleeping well. And if you are not sleeping well because of things like post-traumatic stress disorder, caused by repeated exposure to traumatic events like shootings or violent altercations, then your overall health is surely at risk."

Listening to Terry prompted me to take a deep breath and pay more attention to what was going on inside of me. This was the first time I really began to understand that I was dealing with a problem that was worse than I previously understood, and the stakes could not be higher.

"Let's talk about post-traumatic stress disorder and its connection to mental health and violence. I wrote about this, and I speak about it today because not addressing this issue is harming our community. Folks are dying every day simply because they refuse to get counseling or the treatment they need to heal their lives."

Here's a part of what Terrie wrote in her book about PTSD.

If I saw a kid being brutalized, you know that he was experiencing trauma: it doesn't take a PhD to understand that. But what if you never saw the kid young, and now you see him twenty years later, a grown man, holding down a job, paying the rent, raising a family—all the things that look right on the outside—but that young man is squirming in agony on the inside, still reeling from the aftereffects of that old trauma. Or he doesn't have the outside looking so good, he's dropped out of school and is not working, but still somehow making money, he's making babies and not supporting them, he's in prison or just out, maybe he's peddling the women—and all you see is this angry young man, dangerous not only to those around him but to himself. Hold up a second. Remind yourself that nobody gets that way for no reason. Nobody is "born evil," no matter how many times we might have heard our mothers or grandmothers use that phrase. We are born whole and then life happens. If you see a man who spreads pain everywhere, do not think for a second—no matter how he fronts—that he is not in agony himself. And that brand of agony, more times than not is PTSD.

These words were powerful, and they filled in some of the blanks that I have desperately been trying to fill in for years. Speaking to Terrie allowed me to see my own baggage even more clearly. Also, it gave me a better understanding of Damion and what he may have been going through when we were in prison together. "Hurt people hurt people!" That is how she explained it. When people are hurting inside, there's a strong possibility that without the proper support they will, one day, inflict that same pain or even worse, on someone else.

"Without good mental health, you can't have good health. Not only is the body destabilized and not functioning properly, but when your mental health is off, everything is off. When your mental health is fragile, your entire world is fragile. That is not to say that it cannot be fixed, but at that moment, at that time, you're not the strongest version of you," she said.

In prison, it is relatively normal to talk for hours with the guy you're locked in a prison cell with. There's nowhere to go and not much else to do. It's normal to have conversations about a host of different topics with this person. During our time together, Damion and I talked a lot, and I remember him telling me the story about him being with his friend Keith when he was killed. He told me that he was devastated by that incident, and it was painful to see his friend die in front of him. I remember seeing pain in his eyes as he recanted the story, and I could see that he was scarred by the incident.

After getting a better understanding of trauma and post-traumatic stress disorder, I believe now that Damion may have been suffering from PTSD when we were in prison. His chronic agitation, irritability, hypervigilance, and even his self-destructive behavior, all make sense now. And now the bigger question for me is, did undiagnosed PTSD play a role in Damion murdering Tonessa and Richard?

In hindsight, he had all the classic symptoms of a man struggling with his mental health, but when we were in Allenwood, I did not understand what he was going through. I assumed then that he was just being irrational, immature, and had a bad temper. Back then, I had no understanding of trauma or mental health disorders.

I learned a lot while speaking with Terrie, but ironically, at the end of our conversation I had even more questions than before. Had Damion ever gotten over the trauma of seeing his friend murdered or the mass shooting of twelve people where he was an eyewitness? I'm certain he never received professional counseling after those incidents, because most men wouldn't, including me. We have been conditioned to believe that men are superheroes, and any sign of a struggle with our mental health is a sign of weakness.

Mental health as it relates to violence is a systemic issue, and as a country we have dropped the ball in making sure that all citizens of this country have the resources they need to deal with their illnesses. From Los Angeles to Maine, mental health problems look different in different communities. They attack different age groups and different skin colors in different ways. Mental health issues may also assail a different gender and a different life experience in different ways. Mental health has different voices, and sometimes it may even speak a different language. It's often treated differently by doctors based on a person's class or skin color. But there are also similarities, like, the stigma and the large number of people across America who go undiagnosed each year. And on how mental illness has been researched and treated in minorities, I am sure that decades of structural racism in our healthcare institutions have played a major role in this equation. Like many social determinants where minorities have been negatively impacted, how has this issue been neglected and at what cost?

Several years ago, I was at a conference in Virginia which focused on substance abuse prevention and mental health. I attended the event with staff members from a nonprofit organization I worked for at the time. *Post-Traumatic Stress Disorder* was the term the keynote speaker used repeatedly during her early morning presentation. That was the first time I had ever heard of this term called PTSD, and to be honest, it did not immediately grab my attention.

When violent acts occur on the avenues, streets, and boulevards of our communities, we do not always know where to turn for treatment, counseling, or support. Many of us bury those encounters with violence deep in our psyche, while others self-medicate with alcohol and drugs, as if the pain will be gone in the morning. And some victims of violence go out and commit violent acts themselves, replicating the same misery once inflicted upon them. In urban centers where millions of people live stressful lives, we look at mental health issues as just another bad day in the neighborhood. But the pain is real, and it can leave us screaming silently. Trauma is one of the largest misdiagnosed mental health concerns of our time, and we are far behind other countries in trying to understand it and provide adequate and assessable care.

I remember the very first time I was introduced to extreme violence. It was my indoctrination into gun violence and the trauma that follows. The situation occurred when I was just a sixteen-year-old kid still trying to make sense of this complicated world.

It all started when I got into an argument with a girl, around my same age, who lived in the neighborhood. The argument we had that day was over nothing, and when I say that it was over nothing, I mean absolutely nothing. For some reason, she disliked me, and I disliked her. It was one of those foolish neighborhood disputes that had the potential to explode, and it did.

One bright sunny day she was walking through the neighborhood with a mutual friend of ours that I had a teenage crush on. I was just a teenager, but my testosterone levels were spiking through the roof. Anyway, I looked out of the window and spotted them walking by my house, so I ran outside as fast as I could to catch up with them.

"Hey, what's up!" I said.

"She don't want your skinny ass," my neighbor responded.

I was embarrassed like most teenage boys would be, and I responded like an immature teenager would respond.

"So? Nobody wants your ugly ass either," I said.

Although we did not like each other very much, we had never spoken to each other in that manner before.

"I ain't ugly," she said. "Don't ever call me that again."

She was angry, but I was smiling inside because I thought I was the winner of the verbal jousting against my perceived archenemy.

Then, she fired back, and hard: "Your mother's ugly!"

The verbal dagger went straight through me, and her attempt to damage my ego was achieved. But the rules of verbal jousting are simple: *the last thing you can do is let someone talk about your mother and get away with it. That's a violation of the unwritten rules.* I was embarrassed in front of our mutual friend, the girl I had a crush on, so in my mind I had no choice but to fire back.

"Your mother's ugly...and so is your father and your future kids."

As soon as those words left my mouth, steam began oozing from her big ears.

"Okay. I got something for you! I'm going to tell my boyfriend what you called me!" she said.

But I was not finished, and I had to go there one last time.

"Screw you, your mother, your father, your sister, *and* your chip-tooth boyfriend."

Her face turned flush, and she looked as if she was ready to explode. "Okay, we'll see."

It felt like I had won the war of words, and at the same time, impressed the hottest girl living in the neighborhood. A few hours later, my friend Antonio and I headed off to the basketball court. He loved the game of basketball and so did I. It was summertime and the blazing sun out on the hot asphalt was unforgiving. We were sweating so much that in a short time we were soaked from head to toe. On the court, we made our best impression of Magic Johnson and the Los Angeles Lakers NBA basketball team.

"Shoot the ball, man! You holding up the game!" Antonio yelled.

"Whatever! I hit the last three jumpers," I said.

"No, you didn't!"

We were having fun that day, playing a game that teenage boys and girls all across America love to play. But after competing for a few hours with Antonio, it was time to go home. The only thing on our minds at that point was where to find a tall glass of cold water and some shade.

After we returned to the neighborhood, we were standing on the corner discussing each other's basketball skills, or lack thereof, and where to find a tall glass of water.

"Man, I'm thirsty as hell. My mouth feels like a desert," Antonio said.

"I don't know why. You didn't win nothing," I said.

"Yeah, whatever!"

"The problem is you want to be Magic Johnson, but you can't dribble."

"Whatever."

Then, out of nowhere, the boyfriend of the girl I had been arguing with earlier in the day walked out from behind some tall leafy bushes. He was much older than us, and he was visibly angry. I had completely forgotten about the argument I had earlier that day with my neighbor, but he hadn't.

"Why you messing with my girl?" he said as he slowly approached me.

Antonio and I were both startled.

"What you talking about, man?" I said.

"You said, screw her chipped-tooth boyfriend, right?"

I was immature and trying to be a tough guy, and I inadvertently aggravated an already angry man.

"Yeah, I said it!"

And, under the circumstances, that was the worst possible response a person could give.

He was standing six feet away from me when he pulled out a small silver .22 caliber automatic handgun.

"What you gonna do with that?" I stupidly asked the man holding the gun.

He seemed to be pondering the situation, and since I still had the basketball in my hands, with all the force I could gather, I threw it at his face. Momentarily he was distracted, so, I quickly turned around and ran as fast as I could. Within a second or two, I heard gunshots. *Pop, pop, pop* was the loud sound ringing in the air as he discharged his weapon. I continued running as low to the ground as I could as I weaved around parked cars in the adjacent parking lot.

Within three minutes or so, I made it home where I collapsed on my living room floor. I began making an inventory of my limbs to see if I had been struck by bullets, and to my delight I was unscathed. Physically I was okay, but mentally I was scarred. During the shooting, my friend Antonio ran too, and made it home safely. This was the first time in my young life I had come close to death but thank goodness for swift thinking and thank God for his bad aim. I had been just a few feet away from the shooter when he started firing. I survived the battle, but my psyche was rocked by the senseless violence.

From that day on, I have found any sound that resembles gunshots excruciating to hear. I even began to hate the sound of Fourth of July and New Year's Eve firework celebrations. That incident happened when I was just sixteen years old, and it was the start of me being haunted for decades. Just a few months later I witnessed my first murder when Antonio and I snuck inside a nightclub. A man was shot there and later died. After another two years, I witnessed my second murder when a man was shot in the head in broad daylight in Druid Hill Park in front of scores of witnesses. And yet again, I witnessed my third murder, all before the age of twenty-one years old. From there on I witnessed an avalanche of shootings and violence, and if it wasn't perpetrated against me then it was perpetrated against someone nearby.

The lingering effects of trauma as it relates to violence are not only experienced by US soldiers carrying semi-automatic rifles during war, but they are also a byproduct of the violence here in America. Thousands of innocent people in our country witness violence every day in their cities, towns, and neighborhoods. How often do we think about the grandmother who constantly hears gunshots in her neighborhood and is afraid to leave her home? How often do we think about the young child living in public housing who regularly sees first responders loading the bodies of victims into an ambulance? How often do we think about the girlfriend who was sitting in the passenger seat of the car that was sprayed with bullets and saw her boyfriend succumb to his injuries? How has the mental health of these individuals, the witnesses, and the bystanders been negatively affected?

# CHAPTER 11

# THE CONVERSATION

"Good morning," I said. "I'm trying to locate an inmate by the name of Damion Neal. I need to know which prison he's in."

The woman I was speaking to on the other end of the phone worked for the Delaware Department of Corrections. She responded, "Do you have an inmate identification number for this person?"

"No, Miss, I don't," I replied. "I only have his name and date of birth."

"Well, a birthdate might help. What is it?" she inquired.

I didn't anticipate it being difficult to locate where Damion was serving his time. After all, he had committed the crime in Dover, so he should have been incarcerated somewhere within the Delaware Department of Corrections. There were only a few prisons in the entire state, so he had to be in one of them. With many questions in mind, I figured a trip to Delaware to visit him would be worthwhile.

"Sir, there's no prisoner named Damion Neal being housed within the Delaware Department of Corrections," the woman stated.

"He has to be there. He was sentenced to life a few years ago. Can you please check again?" I requested.

"Hold on, sir," she said.

A few minutes later, the woman returned to the phone. "Sir, I cannot discuss this inmate with you, and I cannot provide you with any information about him. However, you can call this number. Do you have a pen?"

"Yes," I responded.

"Call this number. There's a gentleman in that office who can assist you with your inquiry." I was completely baffled, but I wrote down the information, nonetheless.

After the call, I was dumbfounded. I didn't understand what was happening, as this was not the norm. I couldn't understand the level of secrecy and knew that something was amiss about the situation. In my experience, it's never this challenging to find out where an inmate is serving time in a correctional system. Correctional departments usually make it relatively easy for families, friends, or attorneys to locate them. What made this even more peculiar was when the woman on the phone said, "I can't discuss this inmate with you."

It took me a few weeks to reach someone who could help me locate where Damion was serving his time. Eventually, I learned that he had been transferred out of the state of Delaware and was now at the River North Correctional Center in Virginia. River North was a level four security facility in Independence, near the North Carolina state border. At capacity, the prison housed nearly a thousand inmates.

Even after officials informed me that Damion was serving his time in Virginia, I still wasn't completely sure he was there. Once I received the address to the facility, I wrote him a letter and mailed a few books. I assumed that if he were not there, prison staff would return the packages, but if he were there, then great, he would receive them. I wanted to sit down and talk to him about the events that led to his incarceration, but I also had to be mindful that I should tread lightly, as who was I to judge. He was serving a life sentence and he had more important things to worry about than my opinion.

A few months after mailing the letter and books, I continued to write more letters over the course of about a year. However, I did not receive a response. I continued sending books, recalling the comfort I had found in receiving reading materials during my time in prison. Reading books was my way of mentally escaping the anguish of incarceration, helping me endure the rough weeks, months, and years. But, despite sending additional reading material, there was still no response, leaving me uncertain as to why. The materials were not returned by the post office, indicating that they had been received by someone at the prison. This made me wonder if he simply didn't want to communicate with me—or anyone else, for that matter. Sometimes, when an individual is serving a long prison sentence, it might take a while for them to come to terms with their reality. It might take time for them to accept the possibility that they may never see the outside world again, and communicating with the outside world can sometimes make their reality harder to bear.

In June 2018, I was lying on the floor of my apartment, scrolling through my cell phone while reading emails. Spam and junk mail are so intertwined with other messages that it's easy to miss important communications. Anyhow, I was sifting through messages when I came across one sent by the Virginia Department of Corrections. The email contained a link to an online visitation form, which had to be from Damion because he was the only person I knew incarcerated in Virginia. Without hesitation, I completed the form, which included a request for a criminal background check, and submitted it for processing. The form's notice indicated that it might take up to ninety days for the application to be either confirmed or denied. This surprised me because I had been mailing books and letters to Damion for a while with no response.

About a month later, I received a message on Facebook from a guy who claimed to be Damion's cousin. He provided a telephone number for me to call, and a few hours after receiving the message, I made the call, and we spoke. He informed me that Damion had asked him to reach out to me and that he had received the letters I had sent just before being transferred to another prison in Virginia. He also shared something quite surprising: Damion was undergoing treatment for multiple myeloma and bone cancer. Twice a week, he was transported by prison officials to a hospital for chemotherapy treatments.

And then, a few weeks later...

"Man, you sound the same, bro," Damion said.

"You do too, man!" I replied, and we both began to laugh.

In August of 2018, I had my first conversation with Damion since I left him in the snowy mountains of Central Pennsylvania. I was at the airport, waiting to board a flight to Florida, when he called. Despite our differences during our time at Allenwood, we still held a healthy amount of respect for one another. After talking to him for a few minutes, I realized that he was still the same guy.

"Remember that time you almost got into a fight with that funky guy from Nigeria because he wouldn't take a shower? You were pissed!" he said. I laughed. "Do you remember Belafonte?"

"Yeah."

"I heard he got transferred over to Lewisburg," I said.

"Yeah, that dude loved to gamble," Damion replied.

"I had a tough time tracking you down, bro. I thought you were still in Delaware."

When I first learned that Damion had been transferred out of the Delaware prison system to serve his time in Virginia, I was confused. However, according to him, there was a valid explanation for his transfer.

"Tonessa and Richard both had big families in and around Dover. Tonessa had like twenty-three brothers and sisters," Damion said. "Rick had about ten, and they had around thirty nieces and nephews. Because Delaware is so small, I kept running into them in the joint. A few times it got heated."

According to Damion, there was tension between him and the victim's family members, and on several occasions, he had been threatened. One morning, Damion was on a prison bus with several handcuffed and shackled inmates en route to the courthouse. One of Tonessa's sisters happened to be one of the prisoners on the bus. According to Damion, she initiated a brief conversation with him, but when she realized who he was, she began yelling loudly, "Wait a minute! This motherfucker killed my sister. He killed my goddamn sister!" A correctional officer heard the commotion and moved Tonessa's enraged sister to the back of the bus. Consequently, due to these repeated interactions and concerns for his safety, Damion was transferred out of Delaware to Virginia through an interstate compact agreement. An interstate compact agreement is a process in which one state transfers a prisoner to another state, and the receiving state sends back another inmate in exchange. This explains why, when I initially contacted the Delaware Department of Corrections to inquire about his whereabouts, they were so evasive about where he was being housed.

"Man, her people wanted to kill me."

During our first conversation in years, I had several questions. I wanted to catch up on what had been happening in his life since I last saw him, especially since the murders. He was released from federal prison in 2004, and the murders occurred in the fall of 2008, so there was a four-year span during which he lived between Baltimore and Dover, and a lot had happened.

After a federal judge transferred his probation to Delaware, Damion moved in with his uncle Donnie, who lived near a small Amish community. He stayed with his uncle for seven months, and according to him, it was a rather challenging experience.

"My cousin Debbie lived there too, and she was a paranoid schizophrenic, so we were constantly in conflict. She even pissed on my clothes one day," he said. "Plus, she told my probation officer that I never came home at night, which caused a big mess."

Ultimately, at the direction of his federal probation officer, Damion was forced to move out of his uncle's home.

"One of my first jobs in Dover was working at a rubbish removal company. I liked working there because the owner was a really cool white guy," he added.

Damion attended Delaware Tech Community College, where he studied human services. His goal was to graduate and become a drug and alcohol counselor to help people dealing with addiction. Later, he secured another job working at Delaware State University, where he was responsible for monitoring students living in a co-ed common area on campus.

One evening, one of his co-workers took him to a small gathering to have drinks with some friends, and that's where he first met Tonessa. Their relationship began as a simple friendship, where, according to him, they were just "drinking buddies," but it eventually evolved into something more intimate. Four months after meeting Tonessa, Damion moved in with her and her children, and for almost two and a half years, they lived together.

"Things were fine at first, but then we started to argue a lot," Damion said.

When Damion first arrived in Delaware, he began drinking heavily, almost on a daily basis. In 2006, he was arrested twice within a few weeks for driving while intoxicated. He also got into a violent altercation with two of Tonessa's cousins, which resulted in him being hospitalized for two days with bruises, abrasions, and a mild concussion.

As a consequence of his driving-while-intoxicated arrests, the judge sentenced him to serve sixty days in jail. After his release, his federal parole officer threatened to violate his probation and send him back to Allenwood. However, instead, the probation officer admitted Damion to the Mirmont Treatment Center in Philadelphia for sixteen days, where he received alcohol addiction treatment. The staff there classified him as a "binge drinker" and required him to attend Alcoholics Anonymous meetings every day, sometimes twice a day. After being discharged from the rehabilitation center, his federal probation officer ordered him to attend anger management sessions with a psychotherapist, which he did for several months. During those sessions, the psychotherapist gave Damion a book to read titled *Angry All the Time: Emergency Guide to Anger Control*, which focused on letting go of pent-up emotions. Damion said he read the book cover to cover, and it helped him recognize "old issues" that were "haunting" him. He also mentioned that the book helped him identify some of the irrational thoughts he often had. After several months of one-on-one meetings, the psychotherapist diagnosed him with anxiety, hyperactivity, and insomnia, and recommended that he see a psychiatrist who could prescribe medication. He now admits that he was reluctant to take any medication as recommended and only met with the psychiatrist once.

In 2006, Damion and Tonessa's relationship took a turn, leading to their breakup. Consequently, he moved out of her residence and in with a male friend who also lived in Dover. His friend introduced him to his aunt, named Linda. Shortly thereafter, Damion and Linda began a romantic relationship, and he moved in with her. However, while he was living with Linda, he continued to have a sexual relationship with Tonessa. According to him, he continued to assist her with her children and provide financial support, despite assuming she was seeing other men.

"I figured she was messing with other guys, but I helped her anyway."

Just before being arrested for the murders at General's Greene, Damion impregnated a woman named Laticia, and in 2009, his son Dustin was born at a hospital in Dover. According to Damion, Laticia would visit the detention center with their newborn son initially, but as the years passed, the visits became less frequent. His son is now fifteen years old and lives in Atlanta. His daughter Desia, who he frequently talked about when we were in Allenwood together, is now twenty-nine years old. Despite her father being in prison for over a decade, they still communicate often.

"Was it tough for her when you first got arrested?" I asked.

"Her mother brought her to see me a couple of times when I was in pretrial, but when she left the visiting room, she would cry a lot. She also struggled with what she read online about the case. But as she got older, she began to cope with it better," he said.

There was no doubt in my mind that the time Damion is serving now is eating him up inside. Being in prison for all these years instead of being present in his children's lives has obviously taken a toll on him.

"I fucked up, man. It's as simple as that. There's no excuse for what I did," he said.

"How did you get caught up in this mess, man?" I asked.

According to Damion, on Friday, November 7, 2008, he was having dinner with Linda at a restaurant in Dover. While dining, Tonessa called on his cell phone and asked him if he knew the whereabouts of a man from whom she could buy drugs. Damion told her that he would drive by the area where the man frequented and let her know if he was there. Later that night, Damion tried to call Tonessa to inform her that he didn't see the man in question and to let her know that he needed to pick up his clothes from her house. However, when he called, an unknown man answered the phone and handed it to Tonessa, who then abruptly hung up.

"I didn't know what was going on. All I knew was something wasn't right," he said.

A few seconds later, Damion called back, and Tamika, Tonessa's cousin, answered the phone, telling him that Tonessa had left and gone to the store. But Damion didn't believe her.

"I'm right around the corner," he said. "I'm going to stop by and pick up my clothes."

Damion explained that at that point, he was convinced that Tonessa was not being truthful with him for some reason, but he didn't understand why. He felt that he needed to know whether she was involved with someone else so he could decide whether to end his involvement with her. According to him, he had been providing her with financial support, and in his mind, he believed that there was an expectation of some degree of loyalty.

"What happened when you arrived at Tonessa's house?" I asked.

"No one was there," he said.

When I asked him about the events of the next day, Saturday, November 8, 2008, the morning he got into a physical altercation with Richard, this is how he described it.

"I was a student at Delaware Technical Community College and attended a computer class on Saturday mornings. After class was dismissed, I went to hang out with some friends at an apartment complex. While I was there, I ran into one of Tonessa's nieces who started telling me that Tonessa was dating someone else. She suggested I should stop giving her financial support."

After his conversation with Tonessa's niece, Damion attempted to call Tonessa multiple times from his cell phone, but she did not respond. So, he decided to go to her house again. A friend of his drove him to Tonessa's house and waited outside in the parking lot. Damion said that he got out of the car, walked over to the house, and pounded on the front door while simultaneously calling her cell phone. A few seconds later, he heard someone come to the door, but they did not open it. He assumed it was Tonessa and threatened to kick the door in if she did not open it.

"That's when I kicked it in," he said.

The door was damaged, as was the locking mechanism, so he simply let himself in. He walked into the house and went into the living room where Richard was seated on a couch, and Tonessa was seated across from him on another sofa.

"What's going on?" Damion asked Tonessa.

"What the hell is wrong with you? Are you crazy?" Tonessa yelled.

In the midst of Damion's argument with Tonessa, Richard got up, grabbed Damion by the arm, and led him out of the front door. Once they were outside, they engaged in a physical altercation that lasted for ten to fifteen minutes. During the scuffle, Damion reached for his cell phone and called his cousin.

"Yo, get over to Tonessa's house. I got a problem," Damion said.

Upon hearing this conversation, Richard released Damion, and the altercation ended. Calmer heads began to prevail, and that's when, according to Damion, Richard said, "Man, she's been lying to both of us."

Tonessa was angry with Damion and began yelling, saying that her neighbors were going to call the police if he didn't leave.

"Once everything calmed down, I told Rick I had something inside her house that I needed—a bag of clothes from inside the closet. That's when we went back to the house, and I retrieved my property. After about a minute or so, I came out of the house, got into the car with my friend, and we left."

A short time later, the Delaware State Police responded to Tonessa's home. However, when they arrived, Damion was nowhere to be found. According to Damion he went over to his friend's house, where they drank beer and had a couple of shots of hard liquor. Later in the day, he received a telephone call on his cell from the Delaware State Police. The officer informed Damion that a restraining order had been filed against him and that he needed to come to the police station to sign it. He found the call unusual and decided not to go to the police station. Instead, he called Tonessa to ask if she had called the police on him.

"No, but my neighbor did," she allegedly said.

During their telephone conversation, Damion said Tonessa insisted that Richard would never return to her home. Later in the evening, Damion spoke to Tamika, Tonessa's cousin, again, and she warned him to end his relationship with her.

"A few weeks before the fight with Richard, Tonessa told me that if we weren't going to get back together, she was going to start dating her friend's brother. Not long after that, I ran into her at a friend's house, and she told me that her relationship with her friend's brother had ended. Later, I learned that the man Tonessa was referring to was in prison on a probation violation, and that was the reason why their relationship ended so quickly. It wasn't until that Saturday that I realized the man Tonessa had been referring to was Rick."

"Just a few days before the fight, we had a victory party at her house after Barack Obama won the 2008 presidential election. We even slept together afterward, so, in my mind, we were working on something. I guess we were thinking about getting back together," he said.

When I asked him what occurred during the early morning hours of November 9, 2008, he described the events in detail.

Damion was at Linda's house asleep when she returned home from playing bingo around 2:00 a.m. He woke up and went to the bathroom. When he turned on the light, he noticed the injury to his eye caused by Richard during their physical altercation. When he came out of the bathroom, he noticed there were several missed calls on his cell phone, including calls from Tonessa and the Delaware State Police. He was still agitated and bothered by everything that had happened earlier and called Tonessa.

"What's going on with the police?" Damion said.

"I have company and can't talk right now," she said then abruptly hung up the phone.

That's when Damion decided to go to her house. Since Linda was asleep, he quietly took her car keys and a handgun, believing that he would be back before she woke up. According to him, he wanted to get to the bottom of whether or not Tonessa was asking him for financial support while at the same time seeing another man.

"Around three o'clock, I drove over to Tonessa's house and sat in the parking lot for a while, trying to figure out if I should go inside or not. Then, I knocked on the front door, but no one answered. That's when I tried the doorknob, pushed the broken door open, and went inside."

"Tonessa," he yelled, but there was no response.

"Then, I walked up the stairs to the second floor, and the lights were on in the hallway. I looked into the bedroom, and there was Tonessa in bed with Richard. Once I saw him in the bed, I just snapped."

"What happened next?" I asked.

"Tonessa jumped out of the bed, and we started arguing. It felt so weird with her standing there half-naked in front of this guy. I was having a tough time with that. We had just had sex on those same sheets a few days earlier. The whole situation was crazy," Damion said.

"What did you do after that?" I asked.

"Rick said, 'We need to talk,' and I said to him, 'I told you I don't have a problem with you.' Tonessa said something to the effect of, 'Don't do this,' and that my little goddaughter was asleep in the other room."

Tonessa was upset and continued to yell at Damion. According to him, he became even angrier. Understandably, she was irate that her former boyfriend had literally burst into her bedroom in the middle of the night. Damion said that Richard was squirming around in the bed, trying to cover himself up, and it made him nervous. According to him, that's when he pulled out the handgun.

"Shut up!" he yelled loudly. "Be quiet and let me say what I have to say!"

According to Damion, he discharged one round from the gun into the floor. He claims that he only fired the gun to force Tonessa to be quiet. However, according to him, she was "still arguing," so he stepped closer to the mattress, which sat on the floor because there was no bed frame, and discharged a second round into the mattress. His goal, he says, was to get Tonessa to be quiet. After his second or perhaps third shot, he heard Richard making a hissing sound and thought Richard might have been grazed by a bullet.

"I looked straight at him and didn't see any blood, so I fired another shot into the mattress." From that point onward he said that Richard never moved again.

"I don't remember firing the fifth or sixth shot, but I remember seeing Tonessa's leg 'shake,' and then she sat down on the floor Indian style. That's when she looked at me as if to say, 'Are you crazy?' I asked her whether she would call the police or not, and she said, no. That's when I thought a neighbor might call the cops in response to the gunshots, so I left. I drove about six blocks away, near the Dover Air Force Base, parked, and called her cell phone several times, but she didn't pick up."

When I asked him why he called Tonessa, he said he called because he wanted her to tell Richard that he wanted to meet with him to "talk things over." He also said that he had no idea they were shot because that was not his intention. According to him, his intention was to scare them, not kill them.

After Tonessa did not answer her phone, Damion drove to a friend's house and hid the weapon in the backyard of a nearby home underneath a bush with the intention of picking it up later.

"From there I got on the highway."

At that point, Damion said he drove towards Baltimore with the belief that if someone had, in fact, been shot, he would "already be down there." As he drove south on the highway, he spoke to his cousin Angie on his cell phone and instructed her to call Tonessa. Angie called Tonessa, but no one answered. Then, he spoke to Linda on the phone.

"Where are you?" she said.

Damion told Linda that he was in New York, although he was actually in Smyrna, Delaware. Later that morning, around 10:00 a.m., he received a call on his cell from a friend in Dover who told him that Tonessa and Richard had been shot and that they had passed away. He said his heart dropped.

"I just cried," he said. "I couldn't believe it."

# CHAPTER 12
# THE CONVERSATION II

THIS WAS A DOMESTIC VIOLENCE case that exploded and in the worst possible way. To be totally honest, after Damion described, in detail, how the incident unfolded inside Tonessa's bedroom, it did not sit well with me. I even got a queasy feeling in my stomach as he recounted the story. After hearing his play-by-play of what happened that night, I needed to know if he had any remorse for the crime he had committed. I did not want to hear that he was "sorry," but I needed to be convinced that he truly understood how his actions had permanently damaged many lives.

Before this conversation, I had been unaware of the brutal details, and learning more made me look at the situation through a different lens. I learned things that I had not known even after my meeting with the prosecutor, and I had a problem with them.

Later that night I laid down in bed to go to sleep and replayed the conversation we had in my mind over and over. I kept visualizing the shooting in my head and I realized that my own trauma had been triggered. I kept saying to myself, "You're the journalist. You're not supposed to have any feelings about this." But I couldn't help it. I had become emotionally attached to this tragedy, and I began to realize that might be problematic. I could not help but feel sympathy for the woman who had been murdered in cold blood. I had become conflicted about Damion because this was ugly, and nasty, and if I can be completely candid, it was cowardly.

A few days after my conversation with Damion, we spoke again, and I had more questions. I asked if he felt any remorse and how he now viewed the events that transpired in the bedroom on General's Greene.

Damion said today he understands the value of life even more and that in the past, he had never been a violent person. The time he has spent incarcerated has allowed him to reflect on life's worth, especially since losing his own family members and friends since returning to prison. He said that Tonessa was his friend, and he was close to her family and children. They loved their mother dearly, he said, so he empathizes with what they're going through today. He also acknowledges that they lost their mother due to what he describes as his "cowardice" and "lack of impulse control." He also expressed that Tonessa did not deserve what happened to her, and every day he carries the pain of knowing that he destroyed lives.

"Were you still in love with her?" I asked.

"Yes."

"If, for some reason, you were to get out of prison, what would you do?" I inquired.

"Visit my children, and then, I guess I would find a job, even while I'm fighting cancer."

"Where would you live? Would you return to Maryland, or would you go back to Delaware?"

He responded by saying that he would never return to either place because the painful memories there are too overwhelming. Instead, he would prefer to move to North Carolina and live with his cousin Angie, where he could have a fresh start.

Due to concerns about the spread of the COVID-19 virus, prisoner visits were conducted exclusively through video. When I saw Damion for the first time since the day I had been transferred from Allenwood, it served as a reminder that I could have also been sitting in a cold, dark prison cell serving a life sentence. At one point, my life had been on a similar path before I began to make better choices. During our video visit, we spoke for almost an hour, covering a wide range of topics.

Damion has faced numerous challenges since his return to prison. In 2020, he was transferred once again, this time to Buckingham Correctional Center, located just outside the town of Dillwyn in Buckingham, Virginia. Before this, he had a harrowing experience where he was bitten by a police dog at another prison. That incident prompted him to file a complaint with the Virginia Department of Corrections. The prison had been on lockdown due to staff shortages for two days. When the cell doors were finally opened around five o'clock in the morning, inmates emerged from their cells onto the cellblock. Minutes later they were abruptly told to return to their cells. Damion, who has bone cancer and a compromised immune system, informed a sergeant that he needed to take a shower. However, the officer refused to allow him to do so, resulting in a verbal confrontation that led to the deployment of a police dog. The dog attacked Damion for several minutes, leaving him covered in blood. The incident was captured on prison surveillance cameras, and his complaint ultimately led to his transfer to Buckingham.

On another occasion, while returning to Buckingham after receiving chemotherapy treatment at a local hospital, the van he was in was involved in an accident. Two prisoner transport vans were traveling at high speed, one behind the other, when they collided. The van behind Damion crashed into the rear bumper of his van. Neither of the drivers reported the accident to their supervisors upon returning to the prison.

Damion was only slightly injured, and once again, Damion found himself filing a grievance against corrections officials. Currently, he continues to receive chemotherapy treatments for multiple myeloma and bone cancer. Life expectancy for someone with his diagnosis is only a few years. He hopes to be considered for a stem cell transplant at the University of Virginia Commonwealth, although a decision has not been made. After learning about all the incidents he's been involved in since his reincarceration, I couldn't help but wonder if this was karma leaving its calling card.

During a telephone conversation in 2022, Damion brought up the issue of his sentence, which he still believes is excessive. He strongly believes that the murders were a crime of passion and that he should not have received such a harsh sentence from the state.

"President Biden's son was the Attorney General for Delaware in 2008 when the two murders were committed. Because it was an election year, I think my case became political. Before my arrest, there was another high-profile shooting in Dover where prosecutors lost the case in a jury trial, so they needed a big win."

It's certainly plausible to believe that Beau Biden would have taken an interest in Damion's case. After all, he was the head prosecutor for the state, and Damion's case was high-profile. The case received significant local media coverage, and crime is always a prominent issue during statewide elections. So, yes, his case would have likely been on Biden's radar. Nonetheless, despite Susan Schmidhauser informing me that she had to seek approval from her superiors when considering Damion's plea agreement, I think it's ridiculous to believe that Beau Biden used Damion's case for political gain.

My latest video visit with Damion was uncomfortable for both of us. He appeared emotionally drained and was not in a good mood. But who could blame him, knowing that he will probably spend the rest of his life behind steel bars and concrete? Who would be upbeat, knowing that the only way they might leave the penitentiary is on the inside of a body bag. On November 9, 2008, three people lost their lives, and one of them was Damion Neal. The life he had once known also came to an end on that cold, dark morning in Delaware.

# CHAPTER 13
# TRUTH AND CONSEQUENCES

DAMION NEAL WAS BORN ON July 16, 1977, at Johns Hopkins Hospital in Baltimore, Maryland, and grew up in a crime-ridden, poverty-stricken area of the city. As a child, he enjoyed playing football with his friends at Kirk Field, where a neighborhood league had been established for decades. He also had a fondness for starting his mornings with a big bowl of Apple Jacks cereal. His favorite childhood cartoon was *Fat Albert and the Cosby Kids*. There was a video game arcade close to his home where he and his friends would spend hours playing *Pac-Man* and *Galaga* for just a quarter.

Damion has three brothers and one sister. Unfortunately, one of his brothers was tragically murdered four months before Damion was arrested for homicide in Delaware. His parents were never married, and during his upbringing, his father didn't spend much time with him. His mother struggled with addiction to crack cocaine and lacked steady employment, so the family relied on financial support from social services. As a child, Damion didn't fully grasp the concept of poverty and tended to blame his mother's addiction for their financial troubles. When asked about his relationship with his mother, he simply described it as "rocky." Tragically, his mother battled ovarian cancer and was misdiagnosed at one point, ultimately passing away when Damion was just fifteen years old—a loss he found incredibly difficult to cope with. Sixty days after her death, he was arrested for carrying a handgun and detained at a juvenile detention center. Although a psychological evaluation was scheduled during his stay there, it didn't happen, and Damion doesn't recall why.

In hindsight, Damion wishes he had received grief counseling after his mother's death, recognizing it as a significant turning point in his life. Shortly after she died he experienced a nervous breakdown and was admitted to a psychiatric hospital, where he underwent a series of evaluations over the course of a month. It's worth noting that he began experimenting with alcohol at the age of thirteen, but he didn't drink to excess during adolescence, nor did he perceive his alcohol use as problematic or habitual. However, his relationship with alcohol would later take a turn for the worse.

"My father was diagnosed with HIV when I was young," Damion shared. "Our relationship was strained, so after my mother died, he didn't want me to move in with him. Instead, I moved in with my twenty-two-year-old cousin Angie. She did her best to care for me, but being young herself, she could only provide limited supervision."

He continued, "He was a smart man, but he became addicted to heroin at an early age. He worked for years as a city government employee, repairing sanitation trucks, snowplows, and other city-owned vehicles. While he earned a decent wage, he didn't do much to support me, primarily because of his addiction."

Damion's father is now in his seventies and resides in a senior housing community. They still communicate occasionally, and their relationship has improved. However, the last time he visited Damion was in 2017, mainly due to his age and the distance between them.

Before Damion's trial commenced, the presiding judge, Judge Young, ordered a forensic mental health examination.

Dr. Kenneth Weiss was one of three doctors who conducted these examinations. Dr. Weiss reported to the judge, "Based on the examination and record review, I express the following opinion with reasonable medical certainty: Mister Neal, at the time of the incident, was not suffering from a mental illness or intoxication. His emotions had been inflamed since the day before when he began thinking about the victims, and it is clear to me that this was a situation of ordinary jealousy taken to the extreme. His distress escalated after he was unable to resolve the situation with Ms. Barlow [Tonessa] on the telephone before leaving for her home." Dr. Weiss went on to state that by the time Damion arrived at Tonessa's house on the morning of November 9, and especially after discovering the victims together in bed, he was in a state of extreme emotional distress, or EED.

A second forensic mental health examination was conducted by Dr. Mandell Much, a licensed psychologist. Dr. Much examined Damion twice over a two-day period and noted that during the examination, Damion was initially suspicious and guarded. His mood was anxious and agitated. Dr. Much observed that Damion was "extremely animated throughout the evaluation, often pacing about the interview room as he described both the events surrounding the shooting and other aspects of his history." He also noted that Damion became "overwhelmed with sadness" when discussing Tonessa's death, admitted to having passive suicidal thoughts, and shared that he was experiencing violent and threatening dreams.

Dr. Much also observed "grandiose themes in his thinking" and noted that Damion appeared confused when contemplating whether he was truly capable of committing the murders. He mentioned that Damion used "neologisms," making up words that did not convey their intended meaning.

"This may have been due to his grandiosity, as he might have been attempting to impress this examiner with his intellect." Furthermore, Dr. Much stated that Damion had poor insight into his own behavior, and his judgment was severely impaired. The doctor also noted past identifications of anger control difficulties, guardedness, paranoia, and grandiosity. These seemed to serve as unconscious defenses to mask a fragile self-image with accompanying low self-esteem. Additionally, past diagnoses included depression and alcoholism, with a therapist also considering the possibility of bipolar disorder and narcissistic personality disorder. Dr. Much noted that Damion's psychiatric illness significantly impacted most of his interpersonal relationships, especially intimate ones, and that he harbored pervasive suspicions, mistrusting most everyone and feeling threatened, either physically or emotionally. "His thinking is very paranoid, often believing that others are out to get him," wrote Dr. Much.

Dr. Much asked Damion when did he learn that Tonessa and Richard were dead, to which he responded, "During the drive to Baltimore, a friend called my cell phone and said, 'Tonessa and some dude are dead. They've been shot, and people are saying you did it.'" The doctor noted that at this point in the interview, Damion started crying uncontrollably, a reaction similar to the one observed during the police interrogation video.

Ultimately, Dr. Much diagnosed Damion with depressive disorder, NOS (not otherwise specified), with a consideration of narcissistic personality disorder. He also observed mood swings and the possibility of bipolar disorder. He concluded that at the time of the murders, Damion was operating under extreme emotional distress (EED).

Lastly, Dr. Robert Thompson examined Damion for three hours at the Delaware Psychiatric Center and diagnosed him with alcohol dependence and a personality disorder, NOS with antisocial and narcissistic personality traits.

Dr. Thompson stated to the court, "In the early morning hours of Sunday, November ninth, 2009, Mister Neal awoke and decided to go to Ms. Barlow's residence. At the time, he had a range of feelings and motivations for going to her home. He was angry with Ms. Barlow for notifying the police about the altercation that occurred on November eighth. He wanted to determine whether Barlow had indeed called the police, potentially exposing him to arrest. His anger toward Ms. Barlow stemmed from her involvement with another man while simultaneously seeking financial assistance from him. In Mister Neal's perception, her request for assistance implied a level of commitment, and he felt 'disrespected' by her actions. Additionally, Mister Neal was upset with Mister Tolson for striking him and injuring his eye. He also wanted to investigate Barlow's relationship with Tolson to decide whether to maintain contact or sever ties. His return to Ms. Barlow's residence was driven by a mix of anger, jealousy, consternation, retribution, and a desire to 'get to the bottom' of the situation with Barlow and Tolson."

After a three-hour examination, the doctor concluded that Damion was not operating under extreme emotional distress (EED) at the time of the murders. But despite Dr. Thompson's disagreement with the findings of the other two experts, this set the groundwork for Damion's attorneys to argue at trial that he had indeed been under extreme emotional distress during the shooting. They contended that his charges should be reduced from murder to manslaughter.

Regarding the matter of extreme emotional distress, Delaware law stipulates the following:

> The intentional causation of another person's
> death by the accused under the influence of

extreme emotional distress constitutes a mitigating circumstance. This circumstance results in the reduction of the crime from murder in the first degree, as defined by Section 636 of this title, to the lesser offense of manslaughter. To establish that the accused acted under the influence of extreme emotional distress, it must be demonstrated by a preponderance of the evidence. Additionally, the accused must, by a preponderance of the evidence, provide a reasonable explanation or excuse for the presence of such extreme distress. The reasonableness of this explanation or excuse shall be evaluated from the perspective of a reasonable person in the accused's situation, considering the circumstances as the accused perceived them to be.

Even if this law had been applied in Damion's case and his sentence had been reduced, he still would have faced a lengthy prison sentence for two counts of manslaughter. However, Damion informed his lawyers that he did not want to pursue an EED defense; instead, he wanted to use a Reckless Endangerment defense. He wanted to testify in front of the jury that his intention was only to shoot into the bed near the victims to scare them, with no intent to harm them.

One of Damion's childhood friends who met Tonessa several times while visiting Damion in Dover knows a lot about the case. "To me, Tonessa seemed like a good person. Her spirit seemed genuine, and her demeanor was always pleasant when I was around."

I asked him if he believes that Damion is remorseful for the crimes he committed, and he was adamant in his response.

"Hell yeah!" he said.

After the murders he spoke to Damion several times, and Damion told him that he was extremely sorry for what happened and that he never intended to kill anyone that night.

"Do you think he was still in love with Tonessa when the crimes were committed?" I asked.

"I believe he was."

"Even though he was living with Linda, you still think he was in love with Tonessa?" I asked.

"Yes, he still loved her! He did not mean to kill that woman."

As for Damion's former girlfriend, Linda, they are friends today, despite the tragic events that transpired. Linda visited him a few times while he awaited trial in the detention center, but their relationship was severely strained. Homicide detectives were still contacting her for questioning, and she eventually became a key witness for the prosecution. After the trial, they did not speak for several years because she harbored anger towards him for everything that had occurred.

Linda talked extensively about their relationship, which she said involved occasional outings to dinner and a movie. However, due to her preference for staying at home, they spent most of their time together watching television and enjoying each other's company. She noted that Damion was usually calm and relaxed when in her presence. Nevertheless, she had to address his excessive drinking on several occasions and recognized that he had a serious alcohol dependence issue.

"He drank a lot," she recalled. "Not every day, but frequently. If you're stumbling or falling down, you're drinking too much." She tried to help him detox on a few occasions because she genuinely cared about his well-being.

When asked about Damion's temper, Linda said she never witnessed any issues with his temper, which is why she was shocked to learn about the murders. She even entrusted him to babysit for her grandchildren, nieces, and nephews. They once attended a wedding together in North Carolina, and everyone there had positive things to say about her then-boy-friend. She never saw any signs of violence in him.

Regarding her interactions with the prosecutor after Damion's arrest, Linda mentioned that initially, the state suggested that the murders resulted from a "love triangle" involving her, Damion, and Tonessa.

"The accusation was made during a meeting with the state's attorney, and I became so angry that I stormed out of the office because it sounded so absurd," she explained.

Linda clarified that she had only met Tonessa once, and their interaction was limited to a conversation where Tonessa claimed to still be involved with Damion.

"One day, she confronted me, saying that she was still involved with him. There was no arguing or yelling; it was just a conversation. Prior to that, I had never heard of Tonessa, and that was the first and last time I ever saw her. I had no knowledge of what Damion was doing when he wasn't with me, so characterizing the situation as a 'love triangle' was crazy."

Today, Linda is adamant that Damion was a decent person who, in her opinion, "lost it" for some reason that she still does not understand. She reiterated that she believes that he is remorseful. "I know he's sorry for what he did. There's no doubt in my mind. I still don't understand what was going through his head because he didn't have to do that. He just didn't."

Damion has been back in prison for over a decade now. When I asked him what a typical day looks like for him in prison, he said that it was kind of routine.

"I wake up around six o'clock and stand up for an institution-wide count of all inmates. After the guards make their rounds and the count is confirmed, they return and open the cell doors to let us out. Shortly after that, I'll take a shower and then have breakfast," he said. "Usually, I use the inmate telephones to call Angie. She has serious health challenges now, so I call often just to check on her."

Mail call is conducted around noon, which is when the guards distribute personal mail to the inmates. Since filing two grievances against the Virginia Department of Corrections, he receives more mail from the courts than he has in years. After mail call, lunch is served either in the mess hall or on the cellblock. Damion says that the food at Buckingham is terrible, so he often eats canned mackerel. "After a little spice, some garlic, and a few minutes in the microwave, it's more than just tolerable," he said.

On weekends, Damion calls his son Dustin to see how he is doing in school and in life. He is in high school now and lives in Atlanta with his mother. Dustin is an A-plus student and at the top of his class in academics. Damion has been in prison for his son's entire life, so their relationship is complicated, and it's still a work in progress.

"But as long as his grades are good, I can't complain," Damion said.

Prison officials allow inmates to buy a variety of books and music using a tablet that they have access to. Damion says that he listens to everything from Alicia Keys and Marsha Ambrosius to Mozzy.

"Most of the music these rappers have out nowadays is garbage, so I don't listen to a lot of that, but Nipsey Hussle has some good music."

Damion recently finished reading the *New York Times* bestselling book *White Fragility*, and he says that he enjoyed it. He also read another *New York Times* bestseller titled *Animalkind*, which was authored by the founder of the animal rights group PETA. A few months ago, he received a copy of civil rights attorney Ben Crump's book, *Open Season: Legalized Genocide of Colored People*.

"Now, that book was good. Our generation ain't nothing like how the Black Panthers were back in the day. Nowadays, these guys ain't standing up for nothing, especially when it really matters."

Besides reading and listening to music, some days he goes out into the prison recreation yard to walk the track and get some fresh air.

"Because of my cancer illness, I don't work out much anymore. Some days I attend religious services in the main chapel. I got a television in my cell, so I watch sporting events, news programs, and my favorite show, Court TV." At night he said he watches the BET Network as well as reruns of the popular television series *Law and Order*. He also enjoys watching reruns of the HBO crime drama *The Wire*, which was filmed not far from where he grew up.

Damion's father sends him money once a month, and they occasionally talk on the telephone. Similar to his relationship with his own son, Damion's relationship with his father is also a work in progress. His father is still managing his HIV condition, but he is managing the disease well with the proper medication.

"To tell you the truth, I don't know how he made it this far. But he's still hanging in there."

When I asked him what goes on daily with the other inmates, he had a very sharp response.

"Top of Form

I don't know what's going on with these guys. These dudes don't do nothing but sit around on their ass all day."

"It don't take five years to get a damn GED," he continued, providing more context to his frustration. "My cellmate been in here for thirty-eight years and he's still in a GED program. I can't understand that. When it comes to education the system is in need of serious reform because, as it stands, it ain't helping nobody."

According to Damion, Buckingham Correctional Center offers vocational programs, but most of them are tailored to inmates with short prison sentences. They also have college programs, but inmates are required to cover the costs themselves. Damion believes the public should question where the funding meant to support prisoner education is actually going, as it doesn't appear to be effective.

"If you don't receive financial support from your family and friends on the outside, survival here is nearly impossible. On one hand, they claim they want to rehabilitate us, but on the other hand, they expect incarcerated individuals to pay for their own education, knowing they can't afford it. So, what message are they sending?" he questioned.

Damion wants the public to understand how mental health issues have adversely impacted his life, which is why he has been so transparent about the challenges he has faced. He wants the world to know that without treatment and counseling, the potential for a person's life to spiral out of control, as his has, is very high.

I remember sitting on the phone with Damion and asking him why it matters now how other people view him. "It's not about me anymore, man. My life is over," he said. "It's about the next young motherfucker who's messed up in the head and thinks that he can just run through life without help. Stop and get some help."

It might be easy to think he's only speaking out now because he got caught and wants to get out of prison. However, after years of conversations with him since the incident, where he shared intricate details about both the crime and his mental health struggles, I believe that he wants to make amends somehow for the terrible crime he is responsible for committing.

# CHAPTER 14

# MAN ON FIRE

THE ODOR WAS NAUSEATING AND each time I inhaled, I felt like I wanted to puke. The smell of defecation and urine combined with the stench of humans crammed in prison cells and soaked in perspiration was agonizing. And the noise inside this old, dilapidated jailhouse was almost unbearable. Hundreds of men were caged in like cargo in the hull of a slave ship leaving the Gold Coast en route to the Americas. It was hell on earth, but you adapted in there just long enough to make it out.

This was the inside of a detention center where people accused of committing crimes were warehoused until they either made bail or until their cases were resolved in a court of law. It was a place where a man became a vicious creature—the closest thing to the devil—just to survive. It was an incubator where men mutated and evolved into savages just to cope with the pandemonium around them.

It was midmorning and I was locked inside my cell doing push-ups and sit-ups trying my best to stay fit. That is when I received a visit from an old frail Latino man who walked with a limp. His right arm was disfigured, and the right side of his face was healing from what seemed to be a crude burn. This man looked like he had been through hell and back.

"Kevin," whispered the old man standing on the other side of the steel cell bars. "Watch your back when you come out."

"Why, old man? What's up?" I said.

"A guy, downstairs, named Diego is telling anyone who will listen that he's got a beef with you, my friend."

He was referring to Diego, a Dominican who had an insatiable appetite for robbing and killing dealers. One day me and a few guys decided that he had to go because he was bad for our business. Two weeks later, he showed his face in the neighborhood again and received a beatdown that only lasted a few seconds but sent a stern warning. He also had a concussion, but he was alive, so according to the code of the streets, he had had a fairly good day.

"He's telling guys that he's gonna deal with you, later today. He's saying that a few years ago, your people jumped him."

"Thanks, old man. But why you telling me this?"

"I know a guy who used to hang out with you, Nate from Edmondson Village. You guys used to be tight."

"Nate was a good guy, but still, why you telling me this?"

"Here, take it, and be careful."

The elderly frail man tried to hand me a homemade knife with gray electrical tape wrapped around the makeshift handle. It was a crude jailhouse shank.

"Nah, old man. I don't need that. I'm going home soon."

The detention center was a gladiator school where almost everyone carried some sort of weapon. The place was full of knives, and if the puncture wound from the sharp object doesn't kill you, catching an infection after getting stabbed with a germ-contaminated knife certainly could.

"If I were you, I wouldn't take any chances. The guy's an animal. He'll eat you alive."

The frail man tried to pass the weapon through the bars a second time, and I refused again. "Forget it!" he said in frustration. Then, he limped away.

Finding out that Diego was there inside the prison raised some concern. He was what we called a *chef*, a tyrant who had a thirst for stabbing people, but he was not much of a fighter. I was doing five hundred push-ups a day, so I was in good shape. And besides, who was this frail old man to tell me what to do? He should worry about himself.

Around noon, a correctional officer walked onto the upper tier and opened the cell doors for the inmates who were still locked inside. As I walked out of the cell, I turned to my left and walked down the tier towards the stairwell which led to the lower level. From there, I made my way down the short corridor towards the common area, where inmates watched television and used the pay phones.

As I walked into the common area, I kept my back as close to the wall as possible. I did not want anyone standing behind me because I was not sure who was a friend and who was a foe. Out of the corner of my eye, I spotted my nemesis standing to the side surrounded by four henchmen. They knew that I was not going down easy, and if I was going down at all, we were all going down together. The other thirty inmates seated in the common area felt the tension too and stood up. Slowly, they began parting the seas and making room for the impending melee. That's when I noticed a few freelancers siding with my enemy, but then something happened that was totally unexpected. A correctional officer entered the common area and yelled, "Inmate Diego! Return to your cell and pack your belongings!"

"Why? What's up?" Diego said.

"You're going home, let's go!" the guard said.

Someone had paid Diego's bond, and he was being released. The officer escorted him to his cell, waited there while he packed his personal property, and escorted him out of the housing unit. I wanted to raise my arms in the air and celebrate like a boxer who won a title, but I restrained myself. I was smiling on the inside, but in the presence of my peers, I kept my composure.

Suddenly, the left side of my torso felt like it had been struck by a lightning bolt, and I keeled over in agony. I placed my hand where I felt an excruciating pain and felt moisture. Then I looked down at my palm, and it was covered in blood. I was confused. I grabbed onto the table in front of me to brace myself from tumbling to the floor because my blood pressure was rising, and my vision was beginning to blur. My kidney had been punctured by a sharp object, and I was bleeding profusely. I had just been stabbed.

The second blow struck me in the back, and went straight in, puncturing a lung and creating more internal bleeding. This final blow put me down on the concrete floor where I began to feel cold chills. I also tasted blood in my mouth as it filled my airway. I was fighting to stay conscious. I rolled onto my side and as I turned, I could see my assailant standing there with the bloody homemade knife in his hand. He looked directly into my eyes because he wanted me to know it was him.

"That was for my nephew, Gino. You shot him up in the Bronx, remember?" he said.

It turns out, the frail old man who walked with the limp was the individual who stabbed me. He was also Diego's uncle, and they were working together the entire time. Diego was not released, and the correctional officer who escorted him out of the housing unit was his sister's boyfriend. He too was in on the caper. By removing Diego from the cellblock, they created the perfect alibi for him not to be directly connected to the crime. It was brilliant.

As I lay there on the floor, in a pool of blood, I could sense that the end was near. All I could think about was my family receiving the news that I died inside a filthy prison surrounded by a bunch of degenerates.

Then…I woke up!

I was home in my bed, and it was just another nightmare. Sweat was pouring from my head, and my hand was trembling. The terrible dreams I'd been having for years were back with a vengeance. Several months had gone by and I was sleeping well and there were no signs of the disorder, but then, there it was. The only dangerous thing I'd done in the last fifteen years was feed wild deer at the local park. My world has changed dramatically, so why was I still having these intense dreams?

Back in the day, we never thought twice about engaging in an altercation in the street if we felt we needed to. Back then, if you had a problem with a guy, you handled it; win or lose, you handled it. You couldn't appear to look weak, because you ran the risk of becoming some predator's victim. You did what you thought you had to do to survive. If a guy messed with you, you messed with him, applying double the amount of pressure he tried to apply to you. If a guy pulled a knife, you pulled out whatever you had to defend yourself. If he set fire to your car, you burned down his whole house. That is the dysfunctional world we spent years in, smothered and drowning.

But then you try to walk away from that world and move on because you realize that there is no future there. You cannot raise a family in that environment because you may not live long enough to enjoy it, so you try to change your life. You get married and settle down because you want to be a better person. You stop hanging out in the street and you're home by ten o'clock at night, because you really don't want to die. You want to fly straight and live a righteous life, but there's a problem because that guy is scarred. Not with a physical scar, but a scar nonetheless, and his scar bleeds sometimes. It's not releasing human blood, but it's oozing with the trauma from the past. The fistfights and the rumbles in the jungle used to happen often. He's been exposed to more traumatic events than he can remember. He's seen rivers of blood flow down into the gutter and he's seen the bright red flesh of open wounds. He's experienced the worst of the worst and he's no longer a "normal" guy. In fact, he's not your average guy either, and he never will be because he's psychologically bruised, and he may be self-medicating now with vodka or cannabis. All he ever wanted was to be a stand-up guy, but now he's a guy who cannot sleep at night because he's damaged. From a distance, he looks normal, but on the inside, he's crumbling into small little pieces. And don't believe for a minute that he doesn't know he's messed up, because he does. But the little voice inside of him keeps saying, "somehow, someway, I have to keep going."

The National Library of Medicine defines PTSD as follows: "Posttraumatic stress disorder (PTSD) is a type of anxiety disorder that can occur after experiencing extreme emotional trauma involving the threat of injury or death." This phrase, "The threat of injury or death," is something to which I can personally relate. I spent a significant amount of time witnessing and experiencing violent events, and it eventually took a toll on me. I used to think it was normal to have dreams where villains chased me, to have trouble sleeping, or to wake up in the middle of the night in a sweat. I believed these experiences were something everyone dealt with. It never occurred to me that I might be grappling with a mental health issue related to the trauma I had been exposed to.

My dreams seldom ended on a positive note. Initially, I didn't see this as a problem. They never concluded with me walking off into the sunset hand in hand with a beautiful woman, like in the movies. There were no scenes of me strolling into the Pacific Ocean with my exotic girlfriend. The endings to my mental theater were often dark and dreadful. My nightmares lacked a predictable pattern, sometimes staying dormant for months before resurfacing with even greater intensity. And when they did return, they were uglier and more menacing than before. Sometimes they arrived in clusters, three consecutive nights of torment, like powerful hurricanes battering the Florida coastline.

In search of clarity, I arranged an informal breakfast meeting with a friend who is a psychologist. These issues had been adversely affecting my quality of life for some time. Some days, it felt like I was sleepwalking with my head in the clouds, and there were mornings when it seemed I had not slept at all.

Dr. Steve was an experienced psychologist with nearly forty years of practice under his belt. He was an old-school practitioner, highly respected by his peers, and his credentials spoke volumes. He had a long resume of helping men who had once been broken to become whole again.

We agreed to meet for breakfast at Teavolve Café on the southeast side of town. It was known for serving the best red velvet pancakes in the city. I consider myself a health food enthusiast, but my choice of red velvet pancakes topped with whipped cream that morning might have cast some doubt on my credibility in that area.

"That certainly looks good," Steve remarked.

"Yeah, though not so healthy," I laughed.

It was a Monday morning, and the café was half full. We sat at a table in the back, ensuring privacy for our conversation.

"So, we often hear the term *PTSD*, especially in the context of military veterans returning from war, but what does it really mean?" I asked.

"The key word here is trauma," Dr. Steve began. "We first need to grasp the concept of trauma—something someone experiences that triggers an emotional response."

Traumas are associated with events that are scary, dangerous, or unexpected, causing a person's physiological and psychological systems to be shocked in some way. Some traumas are short-lived, while others have a more lasting impact. The other term in PTSD is *stress*, and the event or situation responsible for the trauma is referred to as a *stressor*. To put it simply, a stressor, like an earthquake, leads to an emotional reaction we call anxiety or fear. So, the words *stressor* and *trauma* may appear synonymous, but there's a distinction. *Trauma* is used to describe an extreme or catastrophic event—something terrifying, dangerous, accidental, involving sexual abuse, or even witnessing a death. It's an event that, once experienced, disrupts our physiological or psychological state. So, we now have two key terms: *trauma* and *stress*. Trauma signifies an extreme, disturbing event.

"The stress part is the reaction that puts a mechanism in place in our body that we experience physiologically or psychologically. Like, we start to sweat, or we get nervous or anxious, or our stomach gets upset."

"Or we can't sleep at night. That kind of stuff?" I asked.

"Yes."

The experience might be in the form of flashbacks, or the person might have troubling thoughts, which can make falling asleep difficult. Or you might feel the need to become super vigilant, which can make falling asleep difficult. For some people, once they fall asleep, they experience serious nightmares, which can be so frightening that the person wakes up, and this makes falling back to sleep difficult.

I explained to Dr. Steve that most of the time I was not sleeping well and sometimes I was not sleeping at all. There have been nights where I don't fall asleep until three o'clock in the morning and then I am back up at seven because I have to work. I try my best not to show that I'm exhausted, but it's tough when you need to engage with people and you're not well rested.

"That can be a problem. Have you considered sleeping pills?" Dr. Steve said.

"I don't do pills, Doc," I said.

"What do you mean you don't do pills? Do they bother your stomach? Because there's medication available that's easy on your stomach."

"I have this thing about taking any drugs. I think I have a phobia about medication. I even struggle to take an aspirin."

"So, that's a totally different topic of discussion," he said. Let's talk about PTSD and normal stress for a second. So, you might have to give a speech to a group of people. The speech is on a topic that you're not familiar with or you are not as comfortable talking about the topic. But you are still committed to giving the speech, or maybe you need to go to a job interview, and you really want the position. The night before the speech or the interview you don't sleep well, and due to the lack of sleep, you're a little cranky with people the next day. Or you have some difficulty concentrating. Asked why you're cranky, for example, you might say, "Well, I didn't sleep well last night, and I'm stressed out about this speech I have to deliver." In these examples, we would call them anticipatory anxiety, or anticipatory stress. When you are in the interview, if you are still stressed out, that's performance anxiety, because you're not on top of your game and you're worried about making a good impression. But it is still stress and it's still real for you. We have all experienced this and it is familiar to us, so we've got stress.

Now, trauma is something that is very scary, and a lot of people have experienced trauma that has not had long-term effects on them. For example, we drive past a car accident where someone was severely injured or killed. That may not affect us, other than when we saw it, we drove past it, and we may even talk about it with others. But in many instances, it has not affected us.

"What if you were in the car when that accident occurred?" I asked.

"It depends," he said.

In a scenario like this there are a lot of factors that are going to be in play. It could be viewed as a trauma, because obviously, it is scary, it is unanticipated, and it is dangerous, because at that moment your life was put in danger. Not everybody who has been in a car accident experiences post-trauma or some type of post-traumatic reaction. So, what if someone is in a car accident, and their life flashed before their eyes, or maybe they had to have emergency responders cut them out of the car and then they're brought to a shock trauma center where there's all this medical stuff going on around them, and it lasts a couple of days? They might be *stressed out* while all of that is happening. It was traumatic, and now they are recovering, but does this mean that person is going to have a post-trauma effect? They might, but the post-trauma effect might be short-lived. So yes, that is a post-trauma, but that does not mean it is diagnosed as post-traumatic stress disorder.

"The next time you get in a car, you're a little more cautious." Dr. Steve said. "You find your foot getting closer to the brake than the accelerator and you drive a bit slower than you did before. But is that, and here comes that keyword, is that a disorder or a normal reaction to a traumatic event? For it to be a disorder, it must interfere with your normal everyday functioning. That's what makes it a disorder. And the symptoms must last for more than a month and be severe enough to interfere with your relationships or your work to be considered PTSD."

"So, the length of time that it lasts makes it a disorder?" I asked.

"Yes," replied Dr. Steve.

"Say you're not sleeping well for a month. You are re-experiencing the symptoms for thirty days straight, and you avoid driving for at least a month. You are anxious all the time for at least a month. So, to be clear, you're experiencing the symptoms for a month. You're having flashbacks, bad dreams, and scary thoughts, things like that. You avoid driving cars now, and you are on edge a lot, which is another symptom. Some people's symptoms usually begin early, within three months of the traumatic incident, but sometimes they can begin years afterward. The timelines are not static; they're fluid for some people. That's why someone might say, 'I'm fine,' when asked two or three months after a traumatic event, but then two years later, they're surprisingly 'not fine' anymore, and they begin experiencing the after-effects of the trauma," he explained.

Dr. Steve also noted that some people recover sooner than others after a traumatic event. So, during the first month, they may experience all the disruptions associated with trauma, and a mental health professional might label it as a "post-traumatic stress response." However, if it's six months or a year down the road, it transitions from being a response to a full-fledged "post-traumatic stress disorder."

"So, to be clear, that's because of the length of time that it lasts?" I clarified.

"Yup. That is the difference between chronic and acute," he affirmed.

"So, let's apply this to the context of violence, not just a car accident. What about people exposed to violence? Are you saying that if those symptoms persist for more than a month in someone who has been shot at, shot, or witnessed a shooting, they could be affected in the same way?" I asked.

"Absolutely," he confirmed.

He went on to discuss how children living in neighborhoods where they are frequently exposed to violence might be affected. These children might see a dead body in the street, hear gunshots at night, or witness people running and chasing each other—a situation that fits the categories of fear and danger, creating a stress reaction. Over time, this stress can become a part of their daily lives. Dr. Steve emphasized that it's unfortunate but not uncommon for children in such environments to become desensitized to these events, making it challenging to identify post-traumatic stress disorder. These are some of the factors a mental health professional would consider when making an assessment. Is the child experiencing sleep disturbances? Is their ability to concentrate at school affected? Are they frequently on edge and easily startled? If the child fits into these categories and others, it will indicate that the environment is adversely affecting them.

Dr. Steve and I also pondered the plight of innocent bystanders who may have been negatively impacted by the violence around them. This includes individuals like the grandmother living in a high-crime neighborhood who has been hearing gunshots there for thirty years. We wondered how such individuals might have been affected, and if they had been misdiagnosed or undiagnosed, where could they turn for help? We rarely openly discuss the average citizen exposed to violence in their own communities. Apart from being a resident there, they have nothing to do with the ongoing violence. But they certainly experience it.

"So, over time, individuals may become desensitized to their surroundings as a coping mechanism?" I asked.

"They absolutely do," Dr. Steve affirmed.

He offered an analogy to help illustrate the concept: "Take, for example, someone who lives in a city with constant vehicle traffic, horns honking, and people talking and yelling at all hours of the night. Can they sleep? Well, if they grew up in that environment, they could sleep. But what if they moved to a rural area where it's quiet, and the only sounds are a couple of crickets? Someone originally from the city might have trouble sleeping there because it's too quiet, and they've become desensitized to noise. Similarly, individuals living near an airport or train station may sleep great because they've become accustomed to the noise and environment. It's akin to the situation with the grandmother living in a high-crime area. She's been exposed to violence for years and can become desensitized."

Another question I had was, could this grandmother also be suffering from some type of trauma or stress reaction?

"The answer is yes," he said.

Here's an example of how the mental health profession has viewed this in the past and how they view it today. After World War I and World War II, soldiers who returned to the states had reactions to the war. Some of them drank heavily, and some were not the same people they had been when they went overseas for combat. I don't mean "the same people" in a positive way, like they got healthier and stronger; I mean they became less functional. There was a term used at the time to describe this, and the term was *shell-shocked*. For example, a former soldier who has returned home walks down the street, and a car backfires, and he immediately ducks for cover. What that says to us is that he was shell-shocked, or traumatized by the explosions and bombs he encountered during the war. If a former soldier ducks for cover when a car backfires or reacts similarly to other loud noises, that person is responding to trauma. It is no different from the grandmother who lives in a high-crime area. If the grandmother suddenly hears a loud noise and she ducks for cover, that means she is also having a post-trauma stress reaction.

When we think of all the people in the United States who have experienced extreme trauma, we know that number is about 7–8 percent of the US population. So, seven or eight out of every one hundred people have, in many ways, been traumatized. Does that mean that 7–8 percent of the population is walking around ducking for cover when they hear a loud noise? Well, it all depends on how well-adjusted or how resilient they are to the trauma they experienced.

There is an adage in the mental health industry that says, "Healthy in, healthy out." So, if somebody is violent, aggressive, and has a propensity for being an anti-social or asocial type of individual—in other words, they don't conform to social norms—and that person has also experienced trauma in their life, will that person be experiencing a post-traumatic stress response? Let's say that person was involved in a shooting, a car accident, or whatever it is; chances are that person is still going to be aggressive afterward. What we're looking for are changes. If I am a normal individual and I am in a car accident, or I am shot, or I experience what we would call trauma (remember, trauma is scary, dangerous, or shocking with a strong emotional reaction), and now I'm not able to perform my everyday activities, like going to work, sleeping well, easily startled, unable to concentrate, always on edge, my social relationships are impaired, and others might tell me that I seem depressed or anxious, I might have a post-traumatic reaction, especially if it lasts for six months or a year. If I am still not functioning well, that is not a post-trauma reaction; that's a disorder.

"I'm saddened and worried that a lot of people, unbeknownst to them, are becoming desensitized to violence, and it becomes their new norm. It's like they have a callous on their emotions," Steve said.

"Like a callous on the hand that thickens just to protect it?" I asked.

"Yes. Their emotions get protected more and more, and that is what that whole desensitization thing is all about," he said.

Becoming desensitized serves as protection against something that can create more anxiety, worry, or fear. If you are not fearful in a healthy way of something that can hurt you, then you leave yourself unprotected. If you are desensitized to pain, and pain is the body's way of saying, "Something's not right, pay attention to me," what happens? Whatever is causing the pain gets worse, and it negatively affects you even more. So, if we take a medical model and say that if I ignore the pain in my chest and pretend that it is not there, then I open myself up for a heart attack. If I ignore the pain in the social system, whether it's an environmental system, a social system, or an emotional system, then I put myself in harm's way of something bad happening.

"We need to acknowledge that people are in pain and hurting. We need to acknowledge that people are in distress or highly stressed on a regular basis. We also must acknowledge that trauma may occur in people's lives and create a readily available system that can help them heal. But without the awareness and without the acknowledgment, then a lot of people are going to have a big heart attack and die unnecessarily," he said.

I was just sitting there in the café, listening to Steve break down this critical information, and I had barely touched the red velvet pancakes sitting in front of me. There is so much the layperson doesn't understand about the issue of mental health. Sometimes I feel like trying to explain it might be useless because if you're not truly committed to learning the information, you will never truly understand it.

"In the world of mental health, what we know now is that a crucial part of the resiliency and healing process, especially within the context of psychotherapy, is the ability to resonate with the person we are speaking to. To resonate, one must have empathy for the individual or the situation," Dr. Steve explained. "Empathy, in essence, means the ability to understand and share the feelings of another in a nonjudgmental way. It's not merely nodding your head and saying, 'I understand.' Empathy should not be confused with sympathy. True empathy is an active approach that conveys not only understanding but also active engagement with the person, recognizing and respecting their resilience. Far too often, people claim, 'I understand you,' when they truly don't. You need to elicit acknowledgment from the person on the other side of the conversation, whether they are across the desk, across the table, or sitting in a chair. You must hear them say, 'Now I know you truly understand me and my pain.'"

Dr. Steve doesn't believe that one must have personally experienced the exact situation as the other person to empathize with them. That would be akin to suggesting that a man could never empathize with a woman who gave birth to a child, simply because men have never undergone that experience. Empathy doesn't require personal experience with a specific situation. With empathy, you can establish a meaningful dialogue and relationship with someone who has encountered a different lifestyle or emotional response to life events, and this, in turn, opens up the potential for change.

"It's a misconception if people believe that they must have lived through the same experiences to connect with others. It all begins with empathy, which serves as the bridge," he emphasized.

"This is deep," I remarked.

"So, did any of this help?" Steve asked.

"It's crazy because you've addressed questions that I've had for years about myself," I replied. "You even touched on some of the things the last therapist I had pointed out."

"Oh, you've been in counseling before?" Steve inquired.

"Yes," I said. "The first psychologist I saw was a prick, but then I met with a guy who told me I might be suffering from PTSD."

Many individuals are grappling with pain both from their past and present-day experiences. And I happen to be one of them. The only reason I'm not sharing a prison cell with Damion today is that I may have been fortunate. Because I also teetered on the brink of destruction, but for some reason, I'm here to share my story.

## CHAPTER 15

# JUST ANOTHER LETTER

Damion,

I hope you're doing well. Just wanted to drop you another letter before I leave town tomorrow. I'm headed to the coast again, but I'll be back next week. Lately, I've been spending a lot of time there to find some peace and quiet to do some writing. The beach has become my personal hideaway, a natural man-cave of sorts. It's the place I escape to when I need to refocus or when the noise in the world becomes too loud. Watching the waves crash onto the sand has a calming effect on me like nothing else. At times, I wonder whether my affinity for the ocean might be linked to my ancestors who endured the Atlantic crossing wearing shackles and chains and perished in the depths of these waters.

When I'm near the water's edge, every part of me feels different—the way my creative mind works, my blood pressure, even my heartbeat. I can't explain why it clears my head and eases my anxiety, but it does. If I had the choice, spending time by the ocean wouldn't just be a refuge for when

I'm overwhelmed; it would be where I would want to live forever.

Something strange happened the last time I was there. It was almost sunset, and I was sitting near a sand dune, watching the waves crash onto the shore. About thirty yards to my right, I saw ten-year-old Kevin Shird sitting alone, staring back at me. It was surreal. I found myself wondering what I would say to young Kevin after causing so much pain in his life. He had so much potential. How could I apologize for all the anguish and agony I caused him with my poor decision making? How could I make amends for what I've done? He was a little kid with big dreams who loved life. He was one of the smartest young men I had ever met who was passionate about math and reading when he was in school. He had a bright future ahead of him, but I just wouldn't get out of his way.

Since leaving Allenwood, I've undergone some very unexpected personal growth. These days, all I want to do is give back to a world I've taken so much from. I want to make a difference, though I'm not always sure what that means. Is making a difference tangible, something you can touch, or is it just a feeling while, in reality, you're just spinning your wheels with no real impact? Sometimes, I'm not sure.

Lately, I've been reflecting a lot on my life. When I first got out of prison, I made some regrettable decisions even when I knew I should not have. I knew I couldn't afford to make any deliberate mistakes, but I did. Frankly, I was disappointed in myself because when you get a second chance, any slip-up can lead to instant condemnation. The mistake I made was befriending someone I shouldn't have, and that decision almost cost me dearly. Even though I thought I had it all together, the truth was that I still had a lot of personal growth ahead of me. But I learned from that experience. From that point on, I made sure my decisions were well thought out and grounded in reasoning.

After that incident, I refocused, and things began going well. I even published three books in just a few years, spoke at a few colleges and universities, and was invited to speak in London. I was enjoying life. Then, within three years, my mother and sister died from cancer, my father had a heart attack and passed away, and a woman I considered a grandmother also died. I thought I was a tough guy, but when the people you love dearly start leaving this world, it changes you and forces you to look at life differently. It felt like it was the hardest three years of my life. But what I came to realize was that I learned a lot from those four individuals, and it was time to apply their lessons. Sometimes, we're moving so fast that we don't realize that the answers we're looking for are right in front of us.

Today, when I watch news programs and see young men who look like us accused of horrific violent crimes, I cringe and change the channel. It's painful when the stories involve individuals who likely struggled with mental health issues long before they committed those crimes. Some people don't like the term "Black on Black crime," and I completely understand why. But sometimes, I struggle to find the right words to describe what's happening in my community with my own people, whom I love dearly.

Some of the same talking heads who take offense at these ideological terms would never stand on a street corner and make the sacrifices needed to end the bloodshed that plagues our communities. Some of them would never walk up to the individuals shooting up neighborhoods, where Black grandmothers and children are trapped in their own homes, and demand that they surrender their weapons. Some of the so-called voices for the people are not genuinely advocating for the community and they're not willing to get their hands dirty. They avoid the most challenging issues where help is needed the most because they often have their own hidden agendas. However, they waste no time rushing in front of a microphone to discuss the violence in the streets while surrounded by personal security.

Sometimes, I wonder if this is the same struggle that literary heroes like Maya Angelou and James Baldwin wrote about when they used finely tuned phrases and eloquent words to express their frustrations with their own communities. I get tired of being politically correct all the goddamn time, and lord knows I don't want to piss off Black Twitter, but enough is enough; somebody has to speak up.

Man, I'm still having these crazy nightmares about being stabbed in prison or being murdered in a cold, dark alley, and it's mind-boggling. A few years ago, I tried to see a therapist and it didn't go well. The guy just sat there staring at me like my head was screwed on backwards or something, so I never went back to see him. But then, I started seeing a therapist over there on East Chase Street and things turned out a lot better. A few years after that, I met a psychologist named Dr. Steve, and we became friends. I never became his client, but I often consulted with him. He was the first white guy I ever met who really understood my journey: the journey of a Black man who was just trying to put the pieces back together.

He helped me understand that writing books, poetry, essays, and other forms of literature serves as a powerful therapy and treatment for trauma victims due to its ability to provide a safe outlet for expression and reflection. Through writing, we can externalize our internal experiences, confronting and processing painful memories in a structured and controlled manner. It allows us to explore complex emotions, untangle thoughts, and make sense of our experiences, fostering a sense of empowerment and agency along our healing journey. Moreover, writing offers a form of validation, enabling people like me to release pent-up emotions and find solace in the act of putting words to our pain. Writing not only facilitates emotional healing but also promotes self-awareness, resilience, and a renewed sense of hope for the future. At that time in my life, that was exactly what I needed. I needed to learn how to breathe all over again.

It's crazy that I'm sitting here writing about this because almost no one knows that I was seeing a therapist. As men we just don't talk about these things the way we should, but it's literally killing us. During a session with this guy, I learned that I might be dealing with something called PTSD, related to my repeated exposure to violence and trauma. One night, I had a dream that I woke up inside a body bag. My legs felt heavy, and they were weighing me down. I desperately wanted to kick my way out of the bag, but my legs wouldn't move. I felt like a cadaver in the morgue, filled with embalming fluid. I could hear people talking about removing my organs and preparing the rest of my body for cremation. I wanted to get out of there, man, but I couldn't. Now that was scary.

Sometimes, I wonder if I was out of my mind when I got involved in the underground drug economy and willingly participated in all the chaos that comes with that world. I question whether I was just another lost soul trying to navigate through the maze. It brings to mind what Grammy Award-winning rapper Nas once said about an innocent, decent kid turning towards crime just to trade his Converse sneakers in for something better.

Some days, I miss the camaraderie of the streets. I don't understand why I miss a place that can show you love one day and kill you the next, but sometimes I do. I realize I may contradict myself at times, but the streets played a significant role in shaping who I am today, and I could never turn my back on the place where I was raised. I just want our people to do better.

In Allenwood, you and I had our differences, but we also had a lot in common. Back then, I saw you as the younger brother who could sometimes drive his older brother crazy. To me, you were like the young sibling trying to carve out a path for yourself in this complicated world. That's how I viewed it back then. I know I got on your nerves at times, urging you to stay out of trouble and keep away from that basketball court, but it was because I cared. It wasn't because I thought I was smarter or better than you; that was never the case. I wanted you to succeed when you got out, and I saw the potential for greatness in you, even when you didn't see it. I recognized your leadership qualities, and I wanted you to thrive. I knew you had that special something that all successful men share—the ability to persuade others to follow them up a steep mountain. But I also saw something else; I saw a young Kevin Shird who had almost ruined his life by making too many poor choices.

In Allenwood, I knew you were wearing the mask because I had firsthand experience with what that looked like. When I talk about wearing the mask, I mean the facade many of us adopt to hide our vulnerabilities and true identity, concealing who we are from the rest of the world. It's easier to wear a mask than to explain to others how complex and quirky we truly are. So, we create a persona that appears menacing and unapproachable, deterring others from messing with us. It's like a "Beware of the dog" sign that convinces others that we're a threat when, in reality, we're just wearing the mask. I'm well aware of the concept of wearing the mask because I wore one for many years. I became a master at concealing my vulnerabilities from others, and it came at a significant cost.

I could tell that you were concealing your true self from the rest of the guys in Allenwood. The only times your true self emerged were when you spoke about the love you had for your daughter. Your eyes would light up when you discussed the person you cared about most in this world. I remember sitting in the cell with you, talking about your plans for when you were released. I remember the big aspirations you had for the future. At that moment, I knew you could achieve them, and your motivation stemmed from your daughter. She was the reason you wanted to do the right thing when you got out. I wonder if she realizes that. I wonder if she knows that, back then, your intentions were those of a father trying to turn his life around for the sake of his child.

The first time I read about what happened in Dover and your involvement in that terrible situation, it was painful to read. Initially, I didn't want to believe it was you. I hoped it was a case of mistaken identity, and there was another guy who committed those crimes, not my old cellmate. I won't deny that I was angry and couldn't believe you would do something like this. However, I eventually realized that holding onto that anger served no purpose. It took me a few years to gain a clear understanding of everything that happened. I know you understand now that you made the biggest mistake of your life, and I believe that if given another chance, you would walk away rather than pull that trigger. But in most tragedies, there are no do-overs, especially when lives have been lost.

I wish I could have been there for you when you needed someone to lean on. In some ways, I feel like I let you down because I know I could have made a difference. I would have known what to say because I remember being in a situation where I almost made a mistake that could have destroyed my life. I vividly recall a moment when I had to choose between walking away and making a disastrous choice.

I wish I could have done something to help you manage your addiction, cope with your mental health issues, and handle the pressures that formerly incarcerated Black men face when reentering society. Looking back, I realize that when we were in Allenwood, you were crying out for help but in your own way. As men, we often wear the mask to conceal our pain and disguise our suffering, even when we know it's tearing us apart inside.

I know you wish you could undo the night when you ended the lives of Tonessa and Richard. I know you well, and I know you were afraid when you fired that gun in that bedroom. But nothing can bring back the mother and father of those beautiful children who will never understand why you pulled that trigger. I still struggle to comprehend what happened on that cold November night. You're the only person alive who was in that bedroom on 2050 General's Way, and you're the only one who truly understands why you made the decision to aim and shoot.

I remember a time when I felt wronged by someone and contemplated seeking revenge. I yearned to release that pent-up anger, to squeeze off a round just to ease the pain. My heart raced, and I could smell revenge in the air. But then, I realized that the pain I felt that day had little to do with the people with whom I was angry. They may have exacerbated my preexisting condition, but they were not the root cause. I was already hurting when they entered my life. My pain ran deep and was embedded in the core of my being, dating back many years. Those old feelings of self-doubt, distrust, and insecurity were staples of my mental health. I had a laundry list of hurt long before I ever met my alleged offenders. They just happened to be there at a time when I was trying to find an antidote for my pain. That day, I was craving an emotional *fix* like an addict, a *fix* in the form of someone else's suffering.

When we were in prison, I knew you were struggling with something, but back then I didn't understand what it was. I was dealing with my own baggage and trying to manage my own mess. Back then, we were all carrying mental baggage, and we were all just trying to survive the time we had to serve in prison. Everyone's emotional mess was weighing them down even while we were trying to hide it from one another.

Earlier in this letter, I mentioned how I used to be a thorn in your side, urging you to stay out of trouble. Back then, I was trying to play the role of a mentor even when I had no idea what that important job really entailed. I realize that the sentence you're serving now must be the hardest thing you've ever had to do in your life. I get it. But there is something you can do that might bring you some peace. I can guarantee that there's a young inmate where you are now who is wearing the mask, concealing his true self, and trying to be someone he is not. Right now, he is grappling with decisions about the direction he should take in his life, probably experiencing many of the same struggles you faced when we first met. What you should do today is make an effort to guide him in the right direction while he's still there. Become a positive influence in that young man's life now, while he still has the chance to change the path he is on. Ask him tough questions like, "Why aren't you taking classes, studying, or reading more books? Do you want to get out and enjoy life with your family or do you want to spend the rest of your days inside the penitentiary, wondering how you messed up so bad?"

# CHAPTER 16
# LIFE PLUS 35

*"I don't know what I would do*
*with a prison sentence that long.*
*I might kill myself."*
—Damion Neal (2003)

I REMEMBER DAMION SAYING THESE words during a long conversation we had back in Allenwood. It was late at night, and we were inside our prison cell talking about inmates like Ace who were serving long prison sentences like fifty years, sixty years, and life. The kind of jail time that would make a man numb inside. Some of those men will be senior citizens by the time they are released, and others will be going home in a coffin.

I remember Damion saying that if he ever had to serve that kind of lengthy prison sentence, he would rather kill himself. When he made that statement, I did not think much about it, until now. It's astonishing to look back at the irony of that conversation, because today he is serving the kind of prison sentence he once said he could not handle: a life sentence.

Damion used to see other inmates who had long prison sentences and would say, "I never want to be like that guy." Well, today he's in prison serving life plus thirty-five years for murder, and he is the guy he once said he never wanted to be.

Today, other inmates may be saying to themselves, "I never want to be like Neal. I don't know what I would do if I had that much time."

As a man evolves, it may take him years or decades to figure out who he really is. It may take him a while to learn how to dig deep down inside to discover what makes him tick, what are his strengths and what are his weaknesses. There is a profound statement written by author Paul Carrick Brunson that goes, "*I didn't find out who I was, until I found out who I wasn't.*"

Damion's legal troubles in Delaware began as a misdemeanor case, where he faced charges of harassment and criminal mischief. Had he made better choices, the situation could have ended there. I am not suggesting that a misdemeanor is not problematic, but instead of the situation ending there, it escalated in the worst way.

The damage to Tonessa's front door on November 8, though unsettling, could have resulted in Damion receiving a reprimand from a Delaware court. Even after his physical altercation with Richard, which was a crime, it remained a misdemeanor charge according to the prosecutor. The case could have likely been resolved with Damion receiving probation and possibly no jail time. He had the opportunity to de-escalate the situation and walk away before it spiraled out of control, but he did not.

Even after he stole Linda's car and handgun, he had moments to reconsider. During his drive to Tonessa's home, he had a chance to pull over and collect his thoughts. He even had the option to turn the car around and return home, but he chose not to. When he entered Tonessa's damaged door, he still had a chance to stop, but something within him prevented him from doing so. He made the fateful decision to enter that bedroom, forever altering not only his life but the lives of countless others.

Damion had a chance to have his charges reduced from first- and second-degree murder to manslaughter, potentially lowering his sentence from life in prison to fifteen to thirty years. He could have been home by now or at least moving in that direction. However, paranoia set in, leading him to believe that his lawyers were sabotaging his case. As a result, he pled guilty to life imprisonment plus an additional thirty-five years. The disorder he suffered from during the murders was still affecting him. His mental instability didn't just vanish on November 9, 2008, the morning of the killings; it continued to influence his decisions, causing him to make more life-altering mistakes.

I'm uncertain if there will ever be activists protesting outside the prison gates, demanding a retrial for Damion. Even though two mental health experts found that he was experiencing extreme emotional distress when he committed the crimes, many people still find his actions reprehensible.

Murder is never a path worth pursuing because if you're caught, and there is a good chance you will be, your life too shall end. It will be like a slow suicide, where you're gradually inflicting pain and suffering onto yourself. Your life will be over because the court system has never been kind to murder suspects, and neither have jurors. For the rest of his life Damion must live with the decision he made that night. He didn't have to kill, but something inside of him drove him over the edge. He had other options that in my opinion weren't hard decisions to make. Any one of those choices would have been better than the one he ultimately acted on. The *universe* understood this and knew that Damion would have to pay a harsh penalty for those transgressions.

In the 2004 movie *Man on Fire*, starring Denzel Washington, the antagonist frequently uses the phrase "*una vida por una vida*" when speaking to John Creasy, the film's protagonist. Translated from Spanish to English, the phrase carries a profound meaning: "a life for a life." Damion Neal took the lives of two individuals, and he would have to surrender his own life in return.

Unfortunately, this isn't solely Damion's story; it's another account of how mental health issues and gun violence are tearing at the fabric of America. It's a narrative that underscores how the culture of violence ingrained in our society is negatively affecting us in ways we are still struggling to understand. How did this man reach a point where he felt he had no choice but to become a cold-blooded murderer? Damion endured adverse childhood experiences or ACEs beginning with neglect by two drug-addicted parents. One parent was addicted to crack cocaine, while the other was addicted to heroin and contracted the HIV virus. According to the Centers for Disease Control and Prevention (CDC), adverse childhood experiences (ACEs) are potentially harmful traumatic events that occur between the ages of zero and seventeen. These events encompass aspects of a child's environment that can undermine their sense of safety, stability, and bonding. Some children are at a higher risk of experiencing one or more ACEs than others. Although all children can be affected by adverse childhood experiences, numerous studies indicate significant disparities in the prevalence of these experiences.

Damion also bore witness to extreme violence, including the murder of his friend Keith, who died in his arms, and a mass shooting of twelve others. His exposure to trauma includes a laundry list of events, and without counseling and the proper treatment he traumatized others, going so far as to murder two innocent people. There's no doubt in my mind that when he discovered Tonessa and Richard together in bed, it triggered overwhelming emotions. It was a classic example of how "hurt people hurt people." And as the old adage in mental health goes, "If you never heal from what hurt you, you'll bleed on (the) people who didn't cut you."

I am by no means making excuses for Damion's reckless behavior. I have daughters, sisters, cousins, and aunts of my own who deserve protection in this violent society where women are far too often unprotected. I'm merely presenting the facts. As author Terrie Williams wrote in her book, *Black Pain*, "Nobody is 'born evil,' no matter how many times we might have heard our mothers or grandmothers use that phrase. We are born whole, and then life happens." If Terrie's statement is factual, then what happened to Damion? How does a man or woman evolve into a cold-blooded killer?

Stories like Damion's, where a person is accused of committing a horrific crime, make it difficult to have conversations with average citizens or politicians about nonviolent offenders and the need for more leniency in nonviolent criminal cases, especially drug offenses. Society tends to lump all criminal defendants together into one big group when that's just not an accurate depiction. Nevertheless, the conversation around the subject of nonviolent offenders becomes convoluted, and that's unfortunate. There is a very distinct difference between a kid selling ten-dollar bags of crack on a corner and a guy who walks into a school with an AR-15 assault-style rifle and kills the innocent.

I spent a total of 4,200 days inside a prison cell, and for what? I was looking for a way to lift myself and my family out of poverty and decided to take a shortcut. But that shortcut exposed me to many things, and it almost cost me my life. Poverty not only represents a profound manifestation of violence but also generates conditions conducive to further violence. Regardless of race, any community confronted with such deprivation inevitably experiences comparable outcomes. Nevertheless, there are consequences for making choices out of desperation: consequences that teach us very hard lessons. I'll never be able to reclaim the years I spent behind bars, but thank God for second chances. I remember walking out of prison, hoping it would be the last time. I remember the uncertainty I felt that day about what life would be like on the other side. The recidivism rate among African American men released from federal prison is the highest in the country, so my concern about returning to the penitentiary was real. Those feelings weren't contrived, unsubstantiated paranoia. I wanted to be the square peg in that statistic's round hole, and I prayed that my fate would be different.

Somedays I feel like I'm suffering from survivor's guilt. It's a condition associated with PTSD where a person feels guilty because they survived a dangerous or deadly situation while others did not. Coming to terms with my personal battle with post-traumatic stress disorder has helped me understand who I am today. I struggled for years with poor sleep habits, as well as anxiety, and I never understood why. Mental health challenges could have easily derailed the progress I made in my return to society. Luckily, I didn't self-medicate with alcohol and drugs like many people suffering from mental health illnesses do when they feel like they need relief. I made a conscious decision to weather the storm, even though I did not understand that the storm never ends if you do not seek counseling and treatment. There are thousands of men and women across the country coping with the same issue and trying to manage it on their own. Many of our military veterans returning home from conflicts overseas struggle with the disorder. Some get counseling and treatment, but many are not so lucky. One of the most important things we can do today is raise public awareness and let people know that they are not alone in their struggle. My hope now is that someone reading this piece of literature is better educated on the issue of mental health. Hopefully, others will decide to seek counseling and a proper diagnosis, so that they too can live a life without the burden of trying to manage this illness on their own.

And I am not going to pretend that I was some innocent bystander out there on the street because there was a time when I was part of the problem and not part of the solution. Accountability matters, and I can only hope that my sins are forgiven. I believe Damion understands that now, but it might be too late.

On a sunny Friday afternoon, I decided to walk from my office to the world-famous Lexington Market. This place has been a mainstay for over a century. When I was a child, my grandmother would place me in the back seat of my grandfather's green Pontiac, and he would drive us to the market. She adored this place because it offered fresh collard greens, yams, lake trout, wild turkey wings, and a variety of other fresh foods. Before my grandmother migrated north to Baltimore with my grandfather in the late 1930s, she lived in South Carolina, where homegrown foods were abundant. So, shopping at the market was like a journey back to the old countryside. She wouldn't leave until stopping by Barron's Delicatessen to purchase delicious Chesapeake Bay oysters or a hot corned beef sandwich on rye, loaded with mustard.

But, on this particular afternoon, I was in Lexington Market to grab lunch before heading to a meeting at City Hall. It was that time of day when the stomach sends a signal to the brain, via neurotransmitters, indicating that it's time to eat. I had a craving for a platter of steamed shrimp from Faidley's Seafood. While I also longed for Charm City's best steamed crabs, I didn't believe the people at my upcoming meeting would appreciate the strong smell of local crustaceans emanating from my clothes. After placing my order, I stood near one of the high-top tables waiting for my food to be prepared. That's when I heard someone yell.

"Kev…what's up?"

I recognized the guy calling me, but I wasn't entirely sure who he was. Then he walked over.

"Bro, what's up?" he asked.

"We were in the joint together, right?" I responded.

"Yeah, man! How you been?"

That's when I realized it was Gee, the guy I used to sit with in the cafeteria at Allenwood several years ago. He was wearing a yellow hard hat and an orange reflective vest, so I assumed he was involved in either utility work or construction. His appearance hadn't changed much, and he still resembled the guy I used to joke around with in the mountains of Central Pennsylvania.

"What you up to these days?" I asked.

"I've been working on a renovation project over on Fayette Street for Turner Construction. Been there for a while. How about you? What you been up to?"

"I've been writing books and working with some non-profit organizations. I go around to colleges speaking to students about staying out of trouble," I replied.

"You an author now?" Gee remarked.

Top of Form

"Yeah."

"Damn, that's what's up! Always glad to see a brother doing well," Gee said.

"When did you get released?" I asked.

"Not too long after you transferred to New Jersey."

"Oh, okay."

"I haven't looked back since. I got off parole a year after that, and I'm loving life, man," Gee said.

"That's cool," I replied.

"Do you remember Belafonte and Eric B?"

"Yeah, how are they doing?" I replied.

"Eric B caught another crack cocaine case two years after he got out. And I heard Belafonte was back in Lewisburg. Did you hear about Rock? He was in Allenwood with us."

"No."

"He's dead, man. They said he came home and started robbing those young boys. One of them caught him coming out of the barbershop and shot him eight times."

"Damn."

"Kev, I'm done with those streets, man. I been working and taking care of my kids. That street shit ain't worth it."

Gee had matured a lot since I last saw him. Ironically, out of all the guys in Allenwood, he was the last one I thought would turn things around. He had been deeply involved in the streets and had a long history of being in and out of prison. But now, he seemed like a completely different person who was committed to doing things the right way.

"Did you ever marry the girl you always used to talk about?" I asked. "The one you were always on the phone with?"

Gee began to laugh.

"Hell yeah!" he replied.

Gee said that getting married was one of the best decisions he had ever made and that his wife was an amazing woman. He also credited her with helping him stay on the right track.

"What about you? Have you tied the knot yet?"

"No! I'm too busy for that."

"If you change your mind, my wife's got some hot friends I can introduce you to."

"No thanks, bro! I'm good. Trust me."

We both laughed.

Gee was enjoying a fulfilling life far from the prison we once shared in Pennsylvania. Even though I was doing well, seeing Gee for the first time in years served as motivation for me. It was another reminder that making good choices will eventually pay off.

"Hey, remember the guy who was in the cell with me? The guy named Damion," I said. "Yeah. What's up with him?" Gee asked.

"He got charged with a double murder up in Delaware."

Gee had the same look on his face that I had on mine the first time I learned the news. It was a look of dismay, but it was also a look of disappointment. Immediately, he understood how serious Damion's situation was, as well as the consequences of such a crime.

"The judge sentenced him to life plus thirty-five. A few years ago, he filed an appeal, but the court denied it," I said.

"Man, that's crazy. But everything happens for a reason, bro. All we can do is pray and continue making the best decisions we can, so we don't end up going down the same path," Gee said.

Just then, the server loudly called out from behind the counter, "Shrimp platter for Kevin!"

"Right here," I yelled as I raised my arm to get the server's attention. Lunch was ready, and it was time to head off to my meeting.

"I need to get out of here, brother. Take care."

"Alright, Kev. You do the same."

As I walked through the bustling downtown streets that afternoon, I realized that running into Gee was a reminder of how lucky I was. It also made me wonder why our transitions from prison back into the community were successful while Damion's was not.

One of the most important lessons I learned throughout Damion's ordeal is that a person may have to figure it out on their own. He or she may have to fight through all the clutter and mental baggage to get to the root of their problem without support because society either doesn't have the wherewithal or the willingness to assist. In the end, it's every individual person's personal responsibility to find a way to fix whatever is broken inside of them, even if that means seeking treatment and counseling. We must find a way to understand the pain and the bad lyrics playing in our heads. We must learn how to turn those agonizing sounds into beautiful music that we can sing, even when our voices tremble.

# EPILOGUE

*A LIFE FOR A LIFE* was written for the homeless, the sick, the poor, and the widowed. It was written for the taxi driver in New York, the waitress in Santa Monica, the seamstress in North Carolina, and the farmer out in Kansas. It is for every man and woman who has ever woken up feeling depressed, anxious, ashamed, or afraid to face the world.

This book is for the layperson, the schoolteacher, the nurse, the bus driver, the alcoholic, the drug addict, the tech worker, and the college professor—those who know something is awry with their mental health but aren't sure what to do. This book is for the woman suffering from depression, the Army veteran coping with PTSD, the accountant with bipolar disorder, and the person recently released from prison, struggling with post-incarceration syndrome (PICS). This book is not just for one individual but for countless people across America who suffer daily from mental health challenges, both mild and severe, and who may not know where to seek help.

When someone wakes up in the morning with a toothache, there's no hesitation about what to do next. Often, it's a visit to the dentist or, at the very least, an effort to ease the pain. However, when it comes to mental health, the stigma surrounding it is so pervasive that when we experience mental agony, we often hesitate to seek help. Many of us do nothing at all while some exacerbate the situation and make it even worse. The stigma around mental health can be suffocating. People often feel ashamed of their struggles—fearing judgment or rejection if they speak up. Mental illness is unfairly seen as a weakness, a flaw, or something to hide from the world. Society has made it hard for those who need help to ask for it, and many suffer in silence, afraid they'll be labeled "crazy" or "nuts." The stigma makes it harder for individuals to seek treatment which sometimes worsens their condition. We must change this narrative. Mental health struggles are not a choice, and they don't define someone's worth. By opening conversations, showing empathy, and educating ourselves, we can break the chains of stigma and create a world where seeking help is seen as an act of courage, not shame.

In 2021, about 57.8 million adults in the United States, or 22.8 percent of the country's overall population, experienced a mental illness. Of these individuals, approximately 14.1 million (around 5.5 percent) were diagnosed with a serious mental illness (SMI), which greatly affects their ability to function in daily life. Mental health conditions impact people across all demographic groups, with the highest prevalence observed in young adults aged 18 to 25. Furthermore, nearly one in two adolescents (49.5 percent) are estimated to have experienced some form of mental disorder during their lifetime. [3] [4] These statistics emphasize the widespread effect of mental health issues in the US and highlight the pressing need for accessible mental health services.

The numbers are staggering, yet as Americans, we find a way to fight through our pain because we are tough and strong, right? But sometimes, being tough and strong isn't enough. Sometimes, we need a helping hand from a professional. Initially, there were two mental health professionals,

---

[3]  National Alliance on Mental Illness (NAMI), "Mental Health By the Numbers," https://www.nami.org/About-Mental-Illness/Mental-Health-By-the-Numbers/

[4]  National Institute of Mental Health (NIMH), "Mental Illness Statistics," https://www.nimh.nih.gov/health/statistics/mental-illness

Dr. Steve and Terry Williams, who became that helping hand for me. They helped me understand PTSD and unresolved trauma in ways I never had before. They helped me understand more about myself as well as Damion.

A comment Terry made in her book, *Black Pain*, still stings to this day: "If you see a man who spreads pain everywhere, do not think for a second—no matter how he fronts—that he is not in agony himself. And that brand of agony, more times than not, is PTSD." This not only reminded me of Damion, and to some degree, myself, but also of countless others. The wealth of knowledge I received from Terry and Dr. Steve was life-altering. It helped me realize how, without proper counseling and treatment, a person can slowly disintegrate and evolve into someone even their family and friends no longer recognize.

The global COVID pandemic brought emotional well-being into the spotlight and encouraged greater transparency. During this time, more people were given the chance to listen to their bodies and openly discuss their struggles. What many of us realized was that we hadn't been doing well for quite some time. This shift in perspective wasn't limited to individuals; employers and institutions, many of which had previously ignored these concerns, also began to address psychological health in ways they never had before.

In recent years, post incarceration syndrome or PICS has gained significant attention from lawmakers. It's described as a set of mental health disorders and emotional challenges that individuals may experience after being released from prison or a long-term incarceration. PICS is often linked to the trauma of being in prison and can resemble other psychological conditions like PTSD, but it is uniquely influenced by the prison environment and the individual's experience within it.

In 2023, US Congresswoman Ayanna Pressley and US Congresswoman Grace F. Napolitano wrote a letter to the

National Institute of Health requesting that more research be conducted around the issue. In the letter, the house members stated, "Throughout the United States, it is critical that we confront barriers that hinder successful reentry for people returning to their communities from carceral settings, including the negative mental health impacts caused by incarceration. We request the National Institute of Mental Health (NIMH) research post-traumatic prison disorder and share findings related to prevention and treatment."

In their letter they also stated, "Every year, more than 640,000 people are released from state and federal prisons. The status of their mental health is a major determinant of what happens next in their journey. Strengthening familial relationships, maintaining steady employment, and developing productive habits require positive mental well-being. Thus, investing in the mental health of the formerly incarcerated population decreases the risk of recidivism and bolsters community safety."

Community safety is closely tied to public safety, and the most effective approach to public safety involves ensuring that individuals have sufficient access to mental health services. According to the Center for Justice Innovation, "Recognizing that things like housing, jobs, and mental health treatment are integral to public safety means pivoting to policies that are *preventative* instead of *reactive*. Instead of responding to crimes only after they have occurred, we can prevent them from happening in the first place by investing in strong, healthy communities." Our criminal legal system impacts a disproportionate number of people struggling with mental health crises. A shocking 54 percent of people in New York City's notorious Rikers Island jails have a mental illness, exacerbated by a lack of access to care as well as inhumane conditions in the jails themselves. Linking people with untreated mental health needs to long-term care in the community—whether or not they have a criminal case—is crucial to lasting public safety.[5]

Over the years, one of the most important lessons I've learned is that life is a series of choices—good and bad. And somedays I wish I could go back into the past and have a conversation with young Kevin; the young Kevin who made some very bad choices. The young Kevin who once believed that the underground drug economy was the only way out of poverty.

Choices, choices, choices—it's a topic that's almost always at the forefront of my mind. These choices are often influenced by how we feel on any given day or in any given moment. Damion made several terrible choices that impacted the lives of many people, including Tonessa and Richard. There's no excuse for his reckless actions, but I can't help wondering: If Damion had received treatment and counseling at an early age, would he have still traveled the path he did? Of course, not every child exposed to trauma and neglect grows up to commit heinous crimes, so what happened?

According to the Center for Disease Control, adverse childhood experiences, or ACEs, are potentially traumatic events that occur in childhood (from birth to seventeen years). Examples of this include experiencing violence, abuse, or neglect, witnessing violence in the home or community or having a family member attempt or die by suicide.

When I was in Allenwood, an inmate named Juan Carlos walked into my prison cell holding a letter in his hand. It was from the federal judge who had sentenced him to twenty years for drug trafficking and conspiracy. He told me he didn't want to read it, fearing it might be bad news. I said, "Well, the only way you're going to find out is to open it."

---

5   "To Achieve Public Safety, Invest in Strong Communities", Center for Justice Innovation *https://www.innovatingjustice.org/articles/what-is-public-safety*

He opened the letter but asked me to read it for him, so I did. Surprisingly, it was good news. The judge was reviewing his appeal and was asking him to submit additional paperwork. I said, "Brother, that's good news!" I explained that the forms he needed were available in the prison law library. Oddly, he didn't seem excited about the news. A short time later, he confessed why. He didn't want to open the letter because he didn't know how to read. Suddenly, everything made sense. He went on to say that he also didn't know how to write, which made it impossible for him to submit the necessary paperwork to the court.

That moment was a turning point in my life. It reaffirmed that acquiring an education was the only way out of the mess I was in. That's why I started working in the prison education building and taking college courses in the first place—I wanted to be around books, and lots of them.

By the time Damion arrived at FCI Allenwood, I had already made up my mind about how I would spend my time in prison: I chose to educate myself. I knew that reading, writing, and taking advantage of the prison education programs would play an enormous role in my survival once I was released.

When I began writing my first book, all the studying and work I previously committed to became invaluable. Every word that landed on the page was birthed through a very unorthodox environment, a federal prison. Every sentence that was constructed was the result of hours spent in the prison library where I learned how to weave together adjectives, descriptive phrases and superlatives to illustrate a thought or a real-life experience. And whether I was writing about Damion or being tormented in my dreams by Diego, every word splashed onto the screen of my HP laptop creating a safe space to speak about mental wellness.

Amid the discord of daily life in America, there exists a quieter, often overlooked reality: the silent suffering of those traumatized by violence. When we speak of violence, it's critical to understand that it's not solely a product of criminal intent but it often emerges from a place of desperation, hopelessness, and unresolved trauma. Individuals suffering from untreated mental health conditions may resort to violence as a coping mechanism or as a way to survive in a hostile environment. Recognizing this, it becomes clear that addressing mental health is not only about personal well-being but also about community safety.

A few years ago, during my visits to Dublin, Ireland, and London, I learned a lot about the United Kingdom. Both cities have a rich culture that dates back many centuries. While in London, I visited Buckingham Palace, the London Bridge, Big Ben, and several other historical sites. The architecture there is truly unique, the people are very welcoming, and the food was incredible. Ironically, it was in London where I had the best Italian food I've ever tasted.

During my time in London, I participated in multiple interviews on the BBC Radio Network. As part of my interview, the host allowed his listeners to call into the radio show to comment on our discussion and ask questions about my first book. Many of the questions revolved around the violence in America. I remember several callers essentially saying that Americans are foolish to allow such easy access to firearms.

"With all due respect," one caller said, "Why is the US so lax about such an important matter? That doesn't make much sense." You know a person is about to express a strong opinion when they begin a question with "with all due respect."

Another listener called into the radio show and said, "Your country is falling apart at the seams. It's unbelievable the amount of carnage that's acceptable there, chap. That would never be tolerated here in the UK." Initially, I didn't fully comprehend where they were coming from, but then the radio host explained to me that England has very restrictive gun control laws, as does Ireland. In fact, in Ireland, there is no such thing as a gun store where people can simply walk in and purchase firearms. Such establishments do not exist. This information was a total surprise to me because I had never heard this before. That's when I responded by saying something like, "Well, we're getting ready to close a loophole on firearm purchases at gun shows." I knew that was a weak response as soon as those words left my mouth. To be honest, I felt like an idiot trying to explain to the English people why America, the superpower of the world, has such lax gun laws.

In England, citizens cannot own handguns or semi-automatic rifles. The only firearms they are allowed to own are manually loaded rifles, shotguns, and long-barreled pistols, and they must be registered with the state. Moreover, not only do you need to pass a lengthy background check before you are allowed to purchase a firearm, but you also need a letter from your doctor. Additionally, owning a gun for the purpose of self-defense is not considered an applicable reason to own a gun there. The contrast between gun laws in America and the United Kingdom is vast. In 2019, only thirty people were killed in the entire country of England as a result of firearms. In Ireland, almost all registered civilian firearms are either sporting shotguns or hunting rifles, and on average, about twelve people per year are killed in Ireland as a result of firearms.

Law enforcement officials alone cannot prevent Americans from killing each other if that is what we want to do, and our religious institutions cannot stop us from killing each other if that is what we choose to do. Common-sense gun policy and smart investment in mental health accessibility is the only thing that can put a stop to the carnage in America.

According to American psychotherapist Peter A. Levine, "the paradox of trauma is that it has both the power to destroy and the power to transform and resurrect." So, at the end of the day just remember, your personal journey towards healing is a process and there is no magic pill. It's one second at a time, one minute at a time, one hour at a time. Healing is reclaiming your power, piece by piece. You've confronted the pain, faced the wounds, and now you will rise stronger. Your journey to wholeness is sacred, and you're worthy of every victory, so cherish them.

# ACKNOWLEDGMENTS

I AM DEEPLY GRATEFUL TO those who have courageously sought mental health counseling and treatment for trauma while showing incredible resilience. Special thanks to my family and friends for their steadfast support, and to my editor for their insightful guidance. A heartfelt appreciation goes to the professionals who dedicate their lives to healing others. This book is dedicated to every single person who fights for recovery and justice and who has illuminated a path forward for all.

# ABOUT THE AUTHOR

Photo by John Bowers

KEVIN SHIRD IS A FOUR-TIME published author, activist, and screenwriter. He has become an expert on using the past to build a better future. Shird began his very unorthodox journey at the tender age of sixteen when he started dealing drugs on the streets of Baltimore. This lead to him serving a total of almost twelve years in prison. Since leaving prison, Shird monetized his life's lesson by authoring books on social issues. He lectures at colleges and universities across America on issues like education, public health policy, and mass incarceration. During the Obama Administration, he collaborated with the White House and President Obama's Clemency Initiative. In 2018, he became an associate at Johns Hopkins University's Center for Medical Humanities and Social Medicine, where he co-teaches a class on public health. Today, he co-teaches a class at Coppin State University.